全国翻译专业本科系列教材

THE SKILLS AND PRACTICE OF INTERPRETING
口译技巧与实践基础教程

李学兵 编著

清华大学出版社

北京

内 容 简 介

本教材以口译技巧为主线编写，共十章。第一章为口译概述；第二章至第十章每章围绕一个口译技巧展开论述，力求讲解完整、全面、透彻。每章设有针对性练习，以专题为副线展开，涵盖众多常见的口译实战话题，如经贸合作、人文交流、医疗卫生等。练习素材不仅来源广泛、语言地道、内容实用，还配有录音（扫码听音），并附有相关的背景知识，以提高学生的多元文化素养。鉴于教材篇幅有限，部分参考译文放在 ftp://ftp:tup.tsinghua.cn/ 供读者下载使用。

本教材可供高校本科英语专业和翻译专业的学生使用，也可作为口译自学者的参考用书。

版权所有，侵权必究。举报：010-62782989，beiqinquan@tup.tsinghua.edu.cn。

图书在版编目（CIP）数据

口译技巧与实践基础教程/李学兵编著.—北京：清华大学出版社，2021.5（2023.9重印）
全国翻译专业本科系列教材
ISBN 978-7-302-54348-0

Ⅰ.①口⋯ Ⅱ.①李⋯ Ⅲ.①英语–口译–高等学校–教材 Ⅳ.①H315.9

中国版本图书馆 CIP 数据核字（2019）第 263198 号

责任编辑：刘　艳
封面设计：子　一
责任校对：王凤芝
责任印制：宋　林

出版发行：清华大学出版社
　　　　网　　址：http://www.tup.com.cn, http://www.wqbook.com
　　　　地　　址：北京清华大学学研大厦 A 座　　邮　编：100084
　　　　社 总 机：010-83470000　　邮　购：010-62786544
　　　　投稿与读者服务：010-62776969, c-service@tup.tsinghua.edu.cn
　　　　质量反馈：010-62772015, zhiliang@tup.tsinghua.edu.cn
印 装 者：三河市春园印刷有限公司
经　　销：全国新华书店
开　　本：170mm×230mm　　印　张：15.25　　字　数：232 千字
版　　次：2021 年 5 月第 1 版　　印　次：2023 年 9 月第 3 次印刷
定　　价：62.00 元

产品编号：073592-01

前　言

《口译技巧与实践基础教程》是本人结合自己多年的口译教学经验、口译理论研究以及口笔译实践经验编写的一本英汉双向口译教材。本教材适合高校本科英语专业和翻译专业的口译课堂教学，也可作为口译学习者自学之用。

口译是一种特殊的跨语言、跨文化交际行为。为了出色完成口译任务，译员除了通晓两门语言之外，还需要具备双语交际能力，掌握口译技能，并拥有良好的心理素质。本着全方位培养学生口译能力的宗旨，本教材以口译技巧为主线，以专题内容为副线，分十章对学生进行训练。教材具有以下主要特色：

第一，编排循序渐进，符合口译过程和口译教学特点。第一章对口译的定义、历史、类型、过程、标准和能力进行概括性探讨。第二章至第十章每章讲解一个口译技巧，依次为：口译听辨理解与逻辑分析、口译的短期记忆、口译与公共演讲、口译的译前准备与预测、口译笔记、句子口译技巧、数字口译、习语口译和口译的应变策略。这种编排方式使教师能够在口译教学中与时俱进，及时增加一些相关话题或热门话题的口译练习，并确保他们能够高效完成教学任务。

第二，内容丰富，选材多样。每章除了讲解、示范口译技巧之外，还设有专项练习和综合练习。大部分练习素材是本人近几年在英国工作期间搜集、整理、编写而成的，涉及教育、文化、互联网、"一带一路"、孔子学院、环境保护、经贸合作、人文交流、医疗卫生等多个话题，力求题材广泛、语言地道、内容实用，并符合时代特点。专题口译还附有相关的词汇和背景知识，旨在帮助学生做好译前准备和提高多元文化素养。

第三，练习形式多样，便于实际操作。练习设计由易到难，从句子、段落到篇章，从视译到听译，从迎来送往交替口译到礼仪祝词及长篇演讲连续口译，再到采访口译，从而多维度帮助学生巩固和掌握所学口译技巧，提高口译能力。口译练习既包括单人练习，又包括小组练习，如两人一组的模拟口译，三人一组的角色扮演对话口译，四人或多人参与的连续口译、情景口译，等等。此外，听译练习均配有录音（扫码听音），便于教师课堂教学和学生课后练习。

随着世界多样化、经济全球化、社会信息化、文化多元化的深入发展，各国之间的联系变得更加紧密，这给口译工作带来了前所未有的机遇和挑战，对译员的口译能力提出了更高的要求。衷心希望本教材能为培养高水平的口译员以及促进不同文化之间的沟通、交流和合作做出贡献。

由于本人水平有限，书中难免存在错漏之处，还望各位同仁和读者批评指正。

李学兵

2021 年 2 月 9 日于伦敦

目 录

第一章　口译概述 ········· 1

1.1 口译的类型 ········· 2
- 1.1.1 交替口译 ········· 2
- 1.1.2 连续口译 ········· 3
- 1.1.3 同声传译 ········· 4
- 1.1.4 耳语传译 ········· 6
- 1.1.5 视译 ········· 7

1.2 口译的过程 ········· 9
- 1.2.1 口译过程三角模式 ········· 10
- 1.2.2 口译多任务处理模式 ········· 10
- 1.2.3 认知三段式口译模式 ········· 11
- 1.2.4 口译阶段模式 ········· 11

1.3 口译的标准 ········· 13

1.4 译员的口译能力 ········· 13
- 1.4.1 双语交际能力 ········· 13
- 1.4.2 口译技能 ········· 14
- 1.4.3 良好的心理素质 ········· 14

第二章　口译听辨理解与逻辑分析 ········· 17

2.1 源语辨析与理解 ········· 17

2.2 注意力与理解 ········· 18

2.3 口译理解公式 ·· 18
    2.3.1 口译的语言知识 ·· 19
    2.3.2 口译的非语言知识 ······································ 33
2.4 口译听辨与逻辑分析 ·· 38
    2.4.1 口译思路归纳分析 ······································ 39
    2.4.2 口译听辨理解分析 ······································ 52

第三章 口译的短期记忆 ·············· 55

3.1 视觉化记忆训练 ·· 55
3.2 概括性记忆训练 ·· 57
3.3 篇章结构程式化记忆训练 ···································· 58

第四章 口译与公共演讲 ·············· 61

4.1 口头表达 ·· 61
    4.1.1 发音 ·· 61
    4.1.2 吐字 ·· 62
    4.1.3 音量 ·· 62
    4.1.4 音调 ·· 62
    4.1.5 语速 ·· 62
    4.1.6 停顿 ·· 63
4.2 肢体语言 ·· 63
    4.2.1 仪表 ·· 63
    4.2.2 身体姿态 ·· 64
    4.2.3 手势 ·· 64
    4.2.4 眼神交流 ·· 64
    4.2.5 面部表情 ·· 65

第五章　口译的译前准备与预测 ······················ 67

5.1 口译的译前准备 ·································· 67
- 5.1.1 长期准备 ·································· 67
- 5.1.2 近期准备 ·································· 68
- 5.1.3 临场准备 ·································· 68

5.2 口译的预测 ······································ 69
- 5.2.1 语言预测 ·································· 69
- 5.2.2 非语言预测 ································ 70

5.3 迎来送往口译 ···································· 71
- 5.3.1 迎来送往译前准备 ·························· 71
- 5.3.2 迎来送往对话口译 ·························· 75

第六章　口译笔记 ······························ 81

6.1 口译笔记特点 ···································· 81

6.2 口译笔记内容 ···································· 82

6.3 如何记口译笔记 ·································· 82
- 6.3.1 口译笔记的符号 ···························· 83
- 6.3.2 口译笔记的缩写 ···························· 86
- 6.3.3 口译笔记样例 ······························ 91

6.4 礼仪祝词口译 ···································· 95
- 6.4.1 礼仪祝词译前准备 ·························· 95
- 6.4.2 礼仪祝词连续口译 ·························· 97

第七章　句子口译技巧 ·························· 99

7.1 句子拆分与合并技巧 ······························ 99
- 7.1.1 主句、从句拆分与合并 ···················· 100
- 7.1.2 并列句拆分与合并 ························ 102

v

- 7.1.3 谓语、非谓语动词拆分与合并 ····················· 104
- 7.1.4 短语拆分与合并 ····················· 106

7.2 词类转换技巧 ····················· 110
- 7.2.1 英语名词转换为汉语动词 ····················· 111
- 7.2.2 英语副词转换为汉语动词 ····················· 111
- 7.2.3 英语介词转换为汉语动词 ····················· 112
- 7.2.4 英语形容词转换为汉语动词 ····················· 113

7.3 环境保护口译 ····················· 114
- 7.3.1 环境保护译前准备 ····················· 114
- 7.3.2 环境保护连续口译 ····················· 119

第八章 数字口译 ····················· 127

8.1 基本数字口译 ····················· 127
- 8.1.1 基数词与序数词 ····················· 127
- 8.1.2 百分数、小数与分数 ····················· 129
- 8.1.3 比率 ····················· 130
- 8.1.4 倍数 ····················· 131
- 8.1.5 不确定数字 ····················· 133

8.2 大数字口译 ····················· 134
- 8.2.1 汉英数字体系对比 ····················· 134
- 8.2.2 大数字口译方法 ····················· 136

8.3 经贸合作口译 ····················· 139
- 8.3.1 经贸合作译前准备 ····················· 139
- 8.3.2 经贸合作连续口译 ····················· 144

第九章 习语口译 ····················· 149

9.1 习语对译法 ····················· 149

9.2 直译法 ····················· 150

9.3	意译法	152
9.4	直译加注法	153
9.5	人文交流口译	157
	9.5.1 人文交流译前准备	157
	9.5.2 人文交流连续口译	160

第十章　口译的应变策略 165

10.1 译员的应变能力 165
10.2 口译的应变策略 165
- 10.2.1 词的处理 166
- 10.2.2 数字的处理 168
- 10.2.3 概括与省略 170
- 10.2.4 语言功能对等 171
- 10.2.5 禁忌话题处理 171

10.3 医疗卫生口译 172
- 10.3.1 医疗卫生译前准备 172
- 10.3.2 医疗卫生连续、交替口译 176

参考文献 187

附录：口译音频实录 191

第一章 口译概述

"口译是一种通过口头表达形式,将所听到(间或读到)的信息准确而又快速地由一种语言转换成另一种语言,进而达到传递与交流信息目的的交际行为,是人类在跨文化、跨民族交往活动中依赖的一种基本的语言交际工具。"(梅德明,2000:6)

口译的历史源远流长,可追溯到人类社会的早期。几个世纪以来,由于宗教传播、航海探索、国际会议等诸多因素的影响,口译应用得越来越广泛。但口译在国际上被认定为一种正式职业始于20世纪初。1919年第一次世界大战结束后,"巴黎和会"的组织者招募一大批专职口译员为会议做交传,此次会议是第一次使用英语和法语两种官方语言进行口译的重要会议。自此,口译的职业性得到认可,自由职业口译员的工作条件得到相应改善,口译的基本方法和技能训练开始受到重视。1927年举行的"日内瓦国际劳工组织会议"首次使用同声传译的模式。第二次世界大战结束后,纽伦堡战犯审判采用的口译模式主要是同声传译。联合国自1945年成立以来,设立了专门的翻译机构,制定了严格的口译员选拔程序。第一所口译学校于1950年在瑞士日内瓦成立。国际会议口译员协会(International Association of Conference Interpreters,简称AIIC)于1953年成立。随着各类全球性和区域性组织的出现,国际交往日趋频繁,口译员扮演着越来越重要的角色。

1.1 口译的类型

根据不同的分类方法，口译可以划分为不同的类型。按其性质分类，口译有三种模式：联络口译、陪同口译和会议口译；按其源语获取方式分类，口译有听译和视译两种模式；按其操作形式分类，口译有五种模式：交替口译、连续口译、同声传译、耳语传译和视译。下面将着重对这五种模式进行阐释和演示说明。

1.1.1 交替口译

交替口译（alternating interpretation）是两种语言之间的交替转换，用于正式或非正式场合中双方对话的翻译。

> 小组练习：三人一组，分别担任中文、英文对话者和口译员，进行交替口译练习。练习时注意转换角色。

练习一

A: How's the weather today?

B: 阴天，怕是要下雨。

A: Do you recommend an umbrella?

B: 最好带上一把。这里的天气多变。一下雨，天气会很凉。多穿点。

A: Sure. I will put on my hat and coat.

B: 但不要担心，我们大部分时间会在室内或车上，在室外的时间不长。

A: That's good.

练习二

A: Beautiful day, isn't it?

B: 是的，这是一年中最好的季节，不冷也不热。

A: It's a perfect day for a walk outside; the air is so fresh.

B: 会谈结束后，我会带您去天安门转一转。

A: That's wonderful. I have long wanted to visit Tian'anmen Square, the center of Beijing.

B: 刚过完国庆节，所有的鲜花、树木等装饰还没有撤掉，您可以大饱眼福。

A: I cannot wait!

练习三

A: It's too hot today. I need a holiday at the seaside.

B: 据说这是伦敦十年来最热的一个夏天。

A: You are right. According to the weather forecast, there are still some hot days ahead.

B: 现在是夏天越来越热，冬天也很少下雪了。

A: That's true. The global warming will bring disasters to the mankind. What's the highest temperature in the summer of Beijing?

B: 近十年的最高温度达到 41℃左右，比伦敦热多了。

A: That is too bad.

1.1.2 连续口译

在进行连续口译（consecutive interpretation）时，译员需要等待发言人讲完一段话、部分内容或全部内容后，才开始翻译。连续口译通常用于会议、研讨会、演讲、发言等场合。

> 小组练习：三人一组，口译下列语段。其中，一人读出源语内容，一人进行连续口译，另外一人对译文进行评价。

练习四

What is American food? At first you might think the answer is easy as pie.

To many people, American food means hamburgers, hot dogs, fried chicken, and pizza. If you have a "sweet tooth", you might even think of apple pie. It's true that Americans do eat these things. But are they the only kind of food you can find in America?

练习五

Except for Thanksgiving turkey, it's hard to find a typical American food. The United States is a land of immigrants, so Americans eat food from many different countries. When people move to America, they bring their cooking styles with them. That's why you can find almost every kind of ethnic food in America. In some cases, Americans have adopted foods from other countries as favorites. Americans love Italian pizza, Mexican tacos, and Chinese spring rolls. But the American version doesn't taste quite like the original!

练习六

中国人崇尚"民以食为天"。中国菜只是一个统称。由于中国幅员辽阔、地大物博，不同的地理环境、多样的气候和丰富的物产形成了当地独具特色的美食和人们特有的饮食习惯。最有影响和代表性的有鲁菜、川菜、粤菜、苏菜、闽菜、浙菜、湘菜和徽菜，即人们常说的中国"八大菜系"。中国人把这些菜系的特点简要地概括为"南甜、北咸、东辣和西酸"。

练习七

尽管各地的饮食口味不同，但中国所有的菜品都讲究色、香、味俱全。烹饪不同的食物需要使用不同的烹饪方法，如煎、炒、炸、炖、蒸、煮等。保留食物的原始风味十分重要；与此同时，人们可以适当添加各种调味料，使菜肴变得咸、甜、酸或辣。目前，中国菜几乎遍布世界各地。许多外国人不仅喜欢吃中国菜，而且还想学做中国菜。

1.1.3 同声传译

在进行同声传译（simultaneous interpretation）时，听与说几乎同时进

第一章 口译概述

行，所以需要有专门的设备。译员坐在隔音的口译厢或口译室里通过耳机接收发言的内容，在听的同时，将发言连续地译成另一种语言后通过麦克风传达给听众。每位听众需要有一个无线接收设备，选择要接收的语种，然后通过耳机接收该语种的发言内容，这一过程一直持续到演讲结束。同声传译多用于大型会议、研讨会或展览会，是目前国际会议上最常用的一种口译模式。有了同声传译，会议可以同时使用多种语言顺利进行。

同声传译通常是2~3人为一组进行连续工作，每15~20分钟换一次人，每工作2~3小时后会休息。当遇到高难度的演讲时，比如发言人的口音过重或是源语的译员太少，同传译员会采取同传接力的方法，即由一组译员把源语译成英语或法语，再由其他译员把译出的英语或法语译成各自的母语。

影子练习（shadowing exercise）是培养同传译员一心多用的有效方法之一，即通过跟读电视节目、广播新闻或其他形式的音频资料进行听说同步练习。口译学习者在进行影子练习时，首先跟读自己的母语，即在过后几秒或几个字词后，立即跟读、复述所听内容；在熟练母语跟读练习之后，再进行外语跟读练习。

> 小组练习：两人一组，交替进行影子练习。一人读出源语内容，另一人进行跟读。

练习八

随着世界多样化、经济全球化、社会信息化、文化多元化的深入发展，人类越来越成为你中有我、我中有你的命运共同体。"一带一路"就是从人类命运共同体的视角出发，倡导共商共建共享的合作理念，通过政策沟通、设施联通、贸易畅通、资金融通、民心相通实现各国共同发展和进步。"一带一路"把欧亚大陆两端，即发达的欧洲经济圈和充满活力的东亚经济圈紧密相连，推动构建公正、合理、透明的国际经贸投资规则体系，促进生产要素有序流动、资源高效配置、市场深度融合，让更多国家和民众体会到实实在在的"获得感"。

练习九

There are three types of couples. The first type is the "calm-calm" couple, in which both members are calm. They almost never fight, almost never get angry, and rarely break up. In contrast, in the "passionate-passionate" relationship, both members are emotional. They often argue and sometimes have fights. However, they tend to be more romantic and try to make up after a fight. As a result, this kind of couple is also likely to stay together. It is the third type of couple, the "calm-passionate" couple, that is most likely to break up. Because one member tends to be calm while the other is passionate, they usually meet the most difficulty. Of course, not all calm-passionate couples have trouble. In some ways, they have the most interesting kind of relationship.

1.1.4 耳语传译

耳语传译（whispering interpretation）类似于同声传译，但通常适用于只有少数或单个人需要翻译的会议或活动。

> 小组练习：三人一组，口译下列语段。其中，一人读出源语内容，一人进行耳语传译，另外一人对译文进行评价。

练习十

I think women are foolish to pretend they are equal to men. They are far superior and always have been. Whatever you give a woman, she will make it greater. If you give her sperm, she will give you a baby. If you give her a house, she will give you a home. If you give her groceries, she will give you a meal. If you give her a smile, she will give you her heart. She multiplies and enlarges what is given to her. So, if you give her any crap, be ready to receive a ton of shit.

第一章　口译概述

练习十一

Shakespeare ever said: "I always feel happy. You know why? Because I don't expect anything from anyone. Expectations always hurt. Life is short, so love your life, and be happy. Keep smiling and just live for yourself. Before you speak, listen. Before you write, think. Before you spend, earn. Before you pray, forgive. Before you hurt, feel. Before you hate, love. Before you quit, try. Before you die, live."

练习十二

友谊像一道彩虹，渲染了我们的生活；友谊像一盏明灯，照亮了我们的灵魂；友谊像一泓清泉，润泽了我们的生命；友谊像一束阳光，温暖了我们的人生。不管岁月如何飞逝，不管经历什么样的人生阶段，真挚的友情永远相伴，给予彼此最温暖的爱的力量。

练习十三

年轻人最大的财富不是他的青春与美貌，也不是他充沛的精力，而是他有犯错误的机会。如果他不能追随自己内心的强烈愿望，去为自己认为该干的事冒一次风险，哪怕是犯一次错误，那么他的青春该是多么苍白！

1.1.5 视译

视译（sight interpretation）是指译员看着源语稿不间断地把源语口头翻译成译入语。视译是同声传译中最常用的训练方法之一。

> 课堂练习：用视译法口译下列句子。

练习十四

1）It is an honor for me to deliver this speech on behalf of the graduating students, and welcome you to this special Commencement Ceremony 2020.

2) I would very much like to extend my personal as well as the collective gratitude from graduating students to Tsinghua University, to the Chinese government, and to this great civilization with the wisdom of self-discipline and social commitment.

3) Tsinghua has been like a mother to us over the past months and years, guiding and nurturing us along the way, providing us with great vision, and placing high expectations on us.

4) Each of us has a different story, including our amazing life experiences and challenges. Please allow me to briefly share with you the course of my journey which has made of me what I am today.

5) I will always remember my mother's teachings, "to complain less and always find solutions at the price of whatever it takes", which brought me to China, an ancient land of new hopes.

6) Over the past years, I have made many friends, including my fellow students, the faculty and staff from my school, and the administrative teams of the university.

7) Every graduating student has his/her own unique experiences and stories, but I believe we all have had a rewarding experience in Tsinghua.

8) They say when you meet the love of your life, time stops, and that's true. What they don't tell you is that when it starts again, it moves extra fast to catch up.

9) Actions speak louder than words. Let us accept new challenges, think beyond our limits, and keep in mind the ethics of life.

10) Let's unite and undertake everything we can for the sake of humanity and the international community. Let's work together for a more promising future and a more prosperous world.

第一章 口译概述

练习十五

1) 我非常高兴也很荣幸能够访问贵校,并与您探讨我们两校之间更密切的合作与交流。

2) 我很高兴向各位介绍我校的历史、现状以及未来十年的目标。

3) 青年一代有理想、有本领、有担当,国家就有前途,民族就有希望。

4) 年轻时荒废了学业的人,不仅失去了过去的时光,而且还葬送了自己的未来。

5) 我谨向今年获奖的同学们表示最热烈的祝贺,并衷心感谢各位老师对他们的悉心指导!

6) 这项比赛已成为国际文化交流领域的一大知名品牌,为各国青年学生了解中国、交流思想、增进友谊搭建起一个完美的平台。

7) 我们需要有能力、有责任心的年轻人来推动人类进步,实现中华民族伟大复兴。

8) 天上不会掉馅饼,努力奋斗才能梦想成真。

9) 语言是了解一个国家最好的钥匙。通过人文交流,中英两国文化中的精华正在对两国人民的思维方式和生活方式产生奇妙的"化学反应"。

10) 中英两国分别是东西方文明的杰出代表,加强彼此语言的学习不仅有利于增进两国民众的相互了解,而且为促进中西方文明互鉴做出贡献。

1.2 口译的过程

口译的任务是帮助说不同语言的双方进行交流。口译并非像表面看到的那样只是听和说,它涉及一个复杂的过程。译员首先要对源语话语信息进行听辨、判断、推理分析、理解、短期记忆和转换,再用译入语表达出来。对口译过程的研究主要有以下四种模式。

1.2.1 口译过程三角模式

巴黎释意学派代表人物 Seleskovitch 和 Lederer（1998）基于口译交际与释意理论解释口译的意义传递现象，将口译作为一种交际活动而不是一种语言符号的转换过程进行研究。该理论的最大特点是对译员的思维过程进行详细描述，提出口译过程三角模式的假说：理解、脱离源语语言外壳与表达，即在理解和表达两个阶段之间还存在着一个意义产生的重要阶段——脱离源语语言外壳。若不能脱离源语语言外壳，意义就不能产生，真正的翻译行为也就无法实现。口译的对象应该是源语信息的意义，而不是其语言形式，意义是语言知识、专业知识、百科知识和交际语境相结合的产物。

1.2.2 口译多任务处理模式

Daniel Gile（2009）的口译多任务处理模式（Effort Models）提出交传和同传的多任务处理模式，强调口译过程中各种注意力之间的竞争和分配以及译员的注意力饱和等假说。Gile 认为在口译过程中，译员的注意力主要分配在三种"活动"（efforts）上，即"听与理解"（listening and analysis effort）、"表达"（production effort）和"记忆"（memory effort）。他用如下公式描述口译交传和同传的过程：

SI（同声传译）= **L + P + M + C**

CI（交替传译）= **L + N + M + C + Rem + Read + P**

L: Listening and analyzing（听与理解）

N: Note-taking（记笔记）

M: Short-term memory operations（短期记忆）

C: Coordination（各方协作）

Rem: Remembering（回忆）

Read: Note-reading（读笔记）

P: Production（表达）

从上述公式可以看出，在口译过程中，译员需要把注意力合理地分配在源语的听与理解、记笔记、短期记忆以及译入语的表达上。如果译员把注意力过多放在表达上，就会影响自己对后面信息的理解和分析，甚至出现漏听，或者没能有效地储存信息的情况。如果译员把注意力过多放在记笔记，或记忆某个信息上，也会影响后续的理解和表达。因此，只有合理分配注意力，译员才能成功完成口译任务。

1.2.3 认知三段式口译模式

当代著名认知心理学家 J. R. Anderson（2014）提出人们从思维到话语全程的认知三段式程序模式，这个模式在口译中的应用体现为：思维构建阶段（structuring stage）——译员要把他人用某种语言表达的思想变成自己完全理解的信息；思维转换阶段（transferring stage）——译员将源语思想转换成译入语的言语形式；思维外化阶段（performing stage）——译员用译入语的言语形式加以表达。

1.2.4 口译阶段模式

Cokely（1992）的口译阶段模式（Cokely's Stages of Interpreting）如表 1-1 所示：

表 1-1　Cokely 的口译阶段模式

Cokely's Stages	Short Description	Reminder
Message reception	The act of physically receiving the source message through the appropriate channel	Perceive
Preliminary processing	The act of recognizing the source message as a linguistic signal	Recognize

（续表）

Cokely's Stages	Short Description	Reminder
Short-term message retention	The act of storing enough of the source signal to achieve an understanding of the message	Chunk
Semantic intent realized	The act of understanding the source message (Importantly, as Cokely [1992: 127] states, "Ideally, of course, the semantic intent of the message realized by the interpreter is that originally intended by the speaker.")	Understand
Semantic equivalent determined	The act of finding equivalents in the target language for the concepts expressed in the source message	Analyze
Syntactic message formulation	The act of (mentally) fashioning an equivalent target message	Formulate
Message production	The act of articulating the target message	Produce

此口译阶段模式更为细化，把口译过程分为七个阶段：感知和理解一个信息的过程发生在前四个阶段，即源语接收（message reception）、初步认知处理（preliminary processing）、储存（short-term message retention）和理解源语信息（semantic intent realized）；言语的产出过程为后三个阶段，即进行分析与语义配对（semantic equivalent determined）、转化成译入语（syntactic message formulation）和进行译入语表达（message production）。

1.3 口译的标准

口译的即时性、现场性、限时性、口语性、跨文化交际性等特点决定了口译的标准为"准""顺""快"。

"准"即准确,是口译首先要遵循的标准,也是最重要的标准。它是指译员在口译过程中准确理解源语信息,忠实谈话双方的本意,全面、完整地传递谈话信息,确保双方的交流顺利进行。虽然口译不可能像笔译那样完美或一字不漏,但重要的、实质性的内容,如人名、职务、机构名称、时间、地点、数字等必须准确无遗漏地翻译出来。

"顺"即通顺,指译员在用译入语表达源语信息时要做到通顺、清晰、流利。译员其实充当了话语双方信息传递的媒介,倘若这个媒介渠道不通畅,甚至在翻译时出现磕磕巴巴的情况,那么必然会影响谈话的整体质量。

"快"即译员反应要快,表达要及时,在翻译的时间把握上遵循又快又好的标准。口译是一种即时性很强的活动,留给译员思考、斟酌的时间极短,讲话人的话音刚落,译员就要开始翻译。这就要求译员的翻译速度一定要快,这样才不会影响双方的交流。

1.4 译员的口译能力

口译是一种特殊的跨语言、跨文化交际行为,译员需要具备多方面能力来完成这一艰巨的交流任务。译员的口译能力可以概括为三方面:双语交际能力、口译技能和良好的心理素质。

1.4.1 双语交际能力

一个合格的译员必须具备至少两种语言之间的交际能力。Bachman(1990:107—108)认为语言交际能力就是把语言知识和语言使用的场景特征结合起来,创造并解释意义的能力。这不是一种单一的能力,而是由几种既有区别又有联系的能力构成的。他提出由语言能力、策略能力和心理机制三部分构成的交际性语言能力的模型。其中，语言能力是指语言组织能力（语法能力和语篇话语能力）和语用能力（社会语言能力和言语施为能力）；策略能力是指在具体情景下运用语言知识进行交际的能力，是一种综合运用已掌握的知识解决问题的能力；心理机制是语言交际时的一种神经和生理过程，如在口译过程中接收源语时使用的视听技能等。因此，译员不但要具备双语语言知识（语音、词义、词汇、句法、语篇等知识），还要具备非语言方面的语用知识，包括文化知识、专业知识和情景知识（对讲话人的背景、谈话内容及对听众的了解），以及运用这些知识进行交际的话语能力和应变能力。

1.4.2 口译技能

口译是"一种综合运用视、听、说、写、读等知识和技能的语言操作活动"（梅德明，2000：8）。Gillies（2013）把口译技能归纳为语言表达（delivery）、听与理解（listening and analysis）、记忆（memory）、记笔记（note-taking）、意义重组（reformulation）、自我监控（self-monitoring）和注意力分配（split attention）。可以说，口译是多项技能的组合，在整个口译过程中，译员应具备听力理解、信息处理以及语言表达能力，其中涉及逻辑分析、短期记忆、记笔记、译数字、意义重组、应变策略、公共演讲等技能。译员需要刻苦训练和长期实践方能熟练掌握这些口译技能。

1.4.3 良好的心理素质

心理素质是在先天素质的基础上，受后天的环境与教育的影响逐步形成的。口译对译员的心理素质提出很高的要求，一方面是因为口译是一种一心多用的语言交际行为，译员需要注意力高度集中来接收和理解源语，进行记忆和意义重组，最后进行译入语的组织与再表达。另一方面，口译是一种面对面的交流，译员有时需要在众人面前完成自己的工作。如果译员的心理素质不过关，出现紧张、怯场的情况，那么他的理解力、注意力、记忆力和快速反应能力都会受影响，进而影响口译质量。在口译过程中，译员良好的心理素质体现在：自信、冷静、能够调控情绪，有较强的心理适应能力和抗压能力，这样才能保证自己思维敏捷、注意力集中、语言表达流畅，并发挥理解力强、记忆力好的优势，从而成功地完成口译任务。

第二章 口译听辨理解与逻辑分析

在口译过程中，译员的首要任务是理解源语。只有完全理解说者的意图，译员才能选择最恰当的字词、最佳的句子结构来进行表达。所以，理解是整个口译过程中十分关键的一步，同时也是一个复杂的过程。下文将从源语辨析与理解、注意力与理解、口译理解公式、口译听辨与逻辑分析四个方面探讨口译过程中的听与理解问题。

2.1 源语辨析与理解

口译的理解始于听觉感知。刘宓庆（2004：87）把口译的"听力"归纳为以下四个方面的能力："（1）前沿听觉能力，特别是 SL（source language，源语）语音信息的准确接收、甄别能力；（2）SL 语音符号的语境化意义的准确解码能力；（3）SL-TL（target language，译入语）词语意义的准确对应能力；（4）作为听觉过程终端的 SL-TL 句法–语义推断、完形能力。"Gile（2009：162）把"听与理解"（listening and analysis effort）定义为："所有与听与理解有关的活动，包括对语音符号的辨析、识别字词的含义和最后决定讲话人所表达的意思。"所以，译员对源语的辨析和理解是一个复杂的认知过程，也可以说是一个"分析、综合的过程，可以分为语言听辨、语法层次分析、语义和篇章分析、文体修辞分析、文化分析、社会心理分析、意义推断和综合"（刘和平，2001：7）。一些心理语言学家认为语言的辨析与理解包括从宏观到微观和从微观到宏观两个过程：前者是根据话语语境、语义和句义进行逻辑推理来辨析言语个体的过程；后者是从辨析声音符号到识别句义，再到建立句子结构，直至理解篇章的过程。

2.2 注意力与理解

鉴于口译的即时性，口头表达的内容在短期记忆中只停留几秒钟时间，可谓转瞬即逝。译员需要高度集中注意力来接收源语信息符号，并进行解码，以达到理解的目的。根据 Gile（2009）提出的口译多任务处理模式可知，在口译时，译员的注意力主要分配在三种"活动"上，即"听与理解""表达"和"记忆"。如果译员在某一方面的注意力多些，那么他在其他方面的注意力就要少些。注意力分配不当会影响译员对源语信息的理解程度。

同时，译员的信息接收不是被动接收，而是一种主动接收。被动接收表现为译员孤立地听入单词和句子，其注意力过多集中在信息的语言形式上。主动接收是指译员非常注意信息的意义，在听的同时主动分析和预测讲话人说了什么，将要说什么，以便跟上讲话人的思路。所以，理解是主动听入的重要条件。只有理解所听信息，译员才能高度集中注意力，跟随讲话人的节奏，抓住讲话内容的思维逻辑。

2.3 口译理解公式

许多翻译专家、译员等都曾强调理解源语不仅需要认知字词和句法结构，还需要译员具备多方面知识。根据 Gile（2009：78—80）的研究，口译过程中的理解因素可以用以下公式表达：

C = KL + EKL + A

C: Comprehension（理解）

KL: Knowledge of the language（语言知识）

EKL: Extra-linguistic knowledge（非语言知识）

A: Deliberate analysis（分析）

=：并非指完全等同，而是指上述三项相互作用的结果。

+：并非算数加法，而是相互作用的介入。

上述公式说明译员需要具备语言知识和非语言知识来理解口译内容，而且语言知识和非语言知识相互依存，互为补充。其中任何一项知识多些，理解效果就更好些；如果某项知识欠缺，另一项知识可以进行补充；如果两项知识都达不到要求，译员有必要进行额外的审慎分析。

扫码观看视频，分析对话双方产生理解问题的原因。

这个视频之所以笑点颇多，是因为双方在对话过程中，出现了理解问题：一是对同音异形异义词的理解错误，Hu 和 who 发音相同，前者是中国姓氏"胡"的发音，后者是英语疑问代词；二是英语连读问题，"Yes, sir."连读听起来像 Yassir，前者是对英语问句的回答，后者涉及历史背景知识，即 Yassir Arafat 是谁；三是 Kofi 和 coffee、Rice 和 rice 两组发音相同但意义不同的词，其中 Kofi 和 Rice 是人名（Kofi Annan 为前联合国秘书长，Condoleezza Rice 为前美国国务卿），而 coffee 和 rice 则为普通名词。这个例子说明理解问题可能源于多个方面，一个合格的译员必须具备语言知识和非语言知识来正确理解源语信息。

2.3.1 口译的语言知识

语言知识是指掌握某种语言，能够表达和接收该语言文字符号并进行交际。它包括对语音、词语、句子及语篇的掌握。

1. 语音

除了单个字词的发音外,对语音知识(phonological factors)的掌握还包括连读、重读、同形异音异义、同音异形异义等。特别是在英语句子中,连读的单词并不总是与单独的单词读音相同。另外,由于重读部分的不同,句子表达的意思也会不同,译员需要格外注意。例如,"I never said he ate your chocolate."这句话,重读落在不同的单词上,表达的意思会不一样。重读第一个单词 I 强调"我从未说过,是别人说的。这个信息'他吃了你的巧克力'可能是真的,也可能不是真的"。重读第二个单词 never 强调"我从未说过,这个信息无论真实与否,我没在任何场合说过"。重读第三个单词 said 强调"我从来没有说过。他可能吃了你的巧克力,但我没说。我也许这么认为,但我从来没有大声说出来(我可能只是暗示过)"。重读第四个单词 he 强调"我没有说是他吃了你的巧克力,但是有人吃了"。重读第五个单词 ate 强调"我没有说他把巧克力吃了。也许他把巧克力拿走扔掉了,或者用它做了别的事"。重读第六个单词 your,强调"他吃的不是你的巧克力,也许是别人的巧克力"。重读第七个单词 chocolate 强调"他吃的不是你的巧克力,而是吃了你的其他东西"。

同形异音异义词,顾名思义,就是那些字形、书写相同但读音不同因而意义也不相同的词语。例如,tear [teə(r)] 是动词"撕裂""拉掉""挣开""拉伤"的意思,而 [tɪə(r)] 是名词"眼泪"的意思;lead [liːd] 是动词"领导""引导""带路""导致"的意思,而 [led] 是名词"铅"的意思;digest [daɪˈdʒest] 是动词"消化""理解"的意思,而 [ˈdaɪdʒest] 是名词"文摘"的意思。又如 content,重音落在第一个音节上为名词,意思是"内容";重音落在第二个音节上为动词或形容词,意思是"满足"。这样的例子还有很多,如 increase、import、export、object 等。

同音异形异义是那些读音相同但书写形式不同因而意思也就各异的词。例如,《爱丽丝漫游记》里有一段爱丽丝和老鼠的对话:

"Mine is a long and sad tale." said the mouse, turning to Alice and sighing.

"It is a long tail, certainly," said Alice, looking with wonder at the mouse's tail, "but why do you call it sad?"

显然爱丽丝没有分清 tale（传说、故事、经历）和 tail（尾巴），使对话有了歧义。这样的例子还有很多，如 brake/break、cell/sell、cent/scent、flour/flower、hour/our、heal/heel、night/knight、hear/here、right/write、son/sun、steal/steel、weather/whether、sole/soul、sea/see，等等。

2. 词语

词语（words and expressions）是词和语的合称，包括单词、词组及整个词汇，是文字组成语句、文章的最小组词结构形式。词的含义包括本义、引申义和比喻义。在一词多义（polysemy）的情况下，一个词可能有多种意思，如果只记住其基本意思，只知其一，不知其二，理解就会出现问题。例如 relation 这个词，既可以表"关系"，也可以是"讲述""叙述"的意思。例如：

- China has established diplomatic **relations** with many countries.

  中国与许多国家建立了外交关系。

- He was the hero according to his own **relation**.

  根据他自己说的，他是个英雄。

另一个容易引起理解问题的是词的搭配（collocations）。英语和汉语都有固定的词组搭配，搭配形式可谓千变万化。同一个词在与不同的词搭配时，会产生不同的意思，有时与其基本意思相差甚远。例如 dry 有"干的""干燥的""干旱的""口渴的""干咳的""无趣味的""枯燥的"等意思，当它与不同的名词搭配时，意思会完全不同。例如：

- dry voice: cold, not expressing emotion（冷漠的、不带任何感情的声音）；
- dry coffee: coffee served without milk and sugar（不加奶和糖的咖啡）；

- dry nurse: a nurse who takes care of but does not breast-feed another woman's baby（照顾婴儿的保姆，相当于中国的月嫂）；
- dry goods: textiles, clothing, threads, elastic, and so on（纺织品）；
- dry bread or toast: plain bread, not covered with butter or jam（不加黄油和果酱的面包片）；
- dry sherry or wine: a kind of wine without a sweet taste（没有甜味的酒）。

又如"快"在英语里是 fast、quick 的意思，但在具体表述中，它有不同的用法。例如：

- 快车：the fast train（不是 the quick train）；
- 快餐：fast food（不是 quick food）；
- 快速冲个淋浴：a quick shower（不是 a fast shower）；
- 一顿快餐：a quick meal（不是 a fast meal）。

在英语中，不及物动词在与不同的介词、副词搭配组合时，可使整个句子的含义发生变化。例如，break 与不同的介词搭配，构成 break away (from)、break down、break in、break off、break through、break up (into)、break with、break out 等词组，因搭配介词的不同，其表达意思也各不相同。另外，have、do 和 make 具有固定的搭配用法，如表 2–1 所示：

表 2–1　have、do 和 make 常用固定搭配

have a bath	do business	make a difference
have a drink	do nothing	make a mess
have a good time	do someone a favor	make a mistake
have a haircut	do the cooking	make noise
have a holiday	do the housework	make an effort
have a problem	do the shopping	make furniture
have a relationship	do the washing	make money

（续表）

have a rest	do your best	make progress
have lunch	do your hair	make room
have sympathy	do your homework	make trouble

无论是英语动词还是汉语动词，当其与不同的名词搭配时，意思会完全不同，如 break 与一些名词构成的搭配有：break the ice、break new ground、break (one's) neck、break (someone's) heart、break someone in 等。汉语搭配的例子也不胜枚举，如有关"吃"的搭配有："吃老本""吃得开""吃豆腐""吃香""吃小灶""吃独食""吃亏""吃醋""吃透精神""吃不饱""吃不消""吃不准""吃心""干什么吃的""吃不了兜着走""吃干饭""吃多了"等。下面这个例子可以帮助我们很好地理解这些词的意思：

- 一位外国领导人访问中国时说，他终于明白了中国文化其实就是"吃文化"。比如：谋生叫糊口，岗位叫饭碗，受雇叫混饭，花积蓄叫吃老本，混得好叫吃得开，占女人的便宜叫吃豆腐，女人漂亮叫秀色可餐，受人欢迎叫吃香，受到照顾叫吃小灶，不顾他人叫吃独食，受了伤害叫吃亏，男女嫉妒叫吃醋，理解深刻叫吃透精神，工作太轻叫吃不饱，负担太重叫吃不消，犹豫不决叫吃不准，敏感多疑叫吃心，不能胜任叫干什么吃的，负不起责任叫吃不了兜着走，办事不力叫吃干饭！我国领导人说："我们应该总结两国关系，你却总结中国文化，是不是吃多了！"

委婉语（euphemism）指用比较温和的词替代粗俗的或使人不愉快的词，用通行的词代替禁忌的词，使表达更加婉转和含蓄，是人们在交际过程中，为了交流顺畅而创造的一种有效的言语表达方式。例如，senior citizens 不是"高级公民"的意思，而是对老年人的尊称。中英文中都有很多委婉语，若译员不能理解其义，就会造成理解问题。如表 2–2 所示：

表 2–2 常用委婉语

中文	委婉语	英文	委婉语
瘸子、瞎子、聋子、傻子、呆子、弱智	残疾人、盲人、聋人、智力障碍者、智障者	the crippled, the blind, the deaf, simpleton	the handicapped, the disabled, the physically-challenged, the intellectually-challenged
老人院	养老院、疗养院、成人之家	old people's home	nursing home, home for adults
保姆	家政人员、保育员	house maid	nanny, housekeeper, nurse, domestic assistant
秘书	行政助理	secretary	administrative assistant
服务员	餐厅管理员	waiter, waitress	dining-room attendant
理发师	发型师、造型师、美容师	hairdresser	beautician, cosmetologist
死	去世、离世、逝世、仙逝、长眠、归西、亡故、捐躯、作古、天年不测、身归泉路、溘然长逝、不在了、永远离开了我们	die	pass away, go to heaven, go west, pay one's debt to nature, be called to God, sleep the final sleep, breathe one's last, meet one's maker, put to sleep

（续表）

中文	委婉语	英文	委婉语
下岗	待业、失业	lose one's job, unemployed	to put one's career on hold, between jobs, to give the pink slip, early retirement, be made redundant
穷	手头不便、囊中羞涩、价格敏感型消费者	poor	be disadvantaged, financially embarrassed
丑、难看	长相一般、相貌平平	ugly	ordinary, plain
胖	结实、富态、丰满	fat	stout, heavyset, plumy, big boned, horizontally challenged
骨瘦如柴、皮包骨头	身材苗条	skinny	slender, slim, willowy, svelte

3. 句子

句子（sentences）是语言运用的基本单位，它由词、词组（短语）构成，能表达一个完整的意思。英语重形合，是一种逐渐从综合型向分析型发展的语言，结构紧凑严密；汉语重意合，是一种以分析为主的语言，结构简练明快。在口译时，译员需要格外注意这两种语言所特有的句式，如汉语的无主句、主谓谓语句、"把"字句、"被"字句、兼语句等；英语的倒装句、省略句、感叹句、祈使句等，以及一些特殊的句式表达。例如：

英译汉

- He didn't speak anything but Greek.

  他只会说希腊语。

- What is a man, but his mind?

  没有头脑者何得称之为人？

- I cannot agree you more.

  我完全同意你的意见。

- We are glad to see the back of him.

  我们巴不得他赶快离开。

- I have other fish to fry.

  我现在很忙，不能做其他的事情。

汉译英

- 他把他人生的黄金时期硬是这样虚度过去了。

  He has squandered the golden years of his life.

- 我被他的事迹深深打动了。

  I was deeply touched by his story.

- 老师让他给家长打电话。

  The teacher asked him to call his parents.

- 很高兴出席今天的晚宴，与大家共庆猪年春节。

  It is a real delight to join you at the banquet to celebrate the Year of the Pig.

- 我亲眼见证了春节成为中英两国人民的节日。

  I have witnessed the Chinese New Year becoming a festival of both the Chinese and British people.

4. 语篇

语篇（discourse）由多个句子组成，其中包括讲话人的相互交流。如果译员不注意上下文中的话语逻辑，如字词的重复、代词或同义词的指代、过渡词等，就有可能抓不住篇章的逻辑思维，从而产生理解问题。在口译实践中，译员还要注意整个语句所涵盖的意向，抓住其暗含的意思（pragmatic meaning），否则就不能正确理解讲话人的原意。例如，"It's very nice talking to you and I hope I haven't disturbed you."（我很高兴与您谈话，希望我没有打搅您。）可能的意向是要结束谈话。

> 课后作业：阅读下列语篇及译文，对比关键词语和典型句子的翻译，并标出过渡词。

练习一

Different Ways to Wish for Good Luck

Throughout different cultures and history, there have always been ways to wish for good luck, from charms to animals, foods, and gestures, all of which can help strike the right note and give the best, sincerest wishes for an auspicious outcome.

There are many traditional lucky charms around the world, most of which are derived from objects in nature. For example, a four-leaf clover symbolizes faith, hope, love, and luck; acorns represent good luck, youthfulness, prosperity, and spiritual growth; amber brings good luck, balances emotions, and eliminates

祈盼好运的各种方法

在不同的文化和历史中，人们总是用不同的方法来祈盼好运，从幸运符到动物、食品和手势，所有这些都可以帮助人们恰到好处地祈求好运，送出最美好、最真挚的祝福。

世界上有许多传统的幸运符，其中大部分来自自然界。例如，四叶草代表信念、希望、爱和幸运；橡子代表幸运、青春、成功与精神成长；琥珀能带来好运，调节情绪，并消除恐惧；星星常用来象征好运，因为在许多古老的文化中，星星可以预测和决定人的命运。除此之外，还有些幸运符是手工制作的。比如，

fear; stars are often used to symbolize luck because many ancient cultures believed that one's fortune could be predicted and controlled by stars. Besides, some lucky charms are made by human hands. For instance, the horseshoe is common in the U.S. as a good luck symbol. People hang it over the door to keep bad luck away and bring good fortune. Keys have been a symbol of fortune and liberation, and three keys kept together symbolize the unlocking of the doors to health, wealth, and love. Coins are considered lucky in many cultures. The exact coin you need for luck can vary, however. In the United States, it is usually the "lucky penny", particularly those that you find facing heads up; in Britain, it is the sixpence coin.

A few animals are specifically tied to the idea of luck or various applications of luck. For example, goldfish are symbols of prosperity, wealth, wisdom, power, longevity, and peace. Dolphins are symbols of luck and protection, as well. This comes from the belief of ancient sailors, who would see dolphins around their

马蹄铁在美国被普遍视为好运的象征。人们把它悬挂在门上，以驱除厄运，带来好运。钥匙一直是财富和自由的象征，三把钥匙放在一起象征着打开了通往健康、财富和爱情的大门。很多文化认为硬币能带来好运，但代表幸运的硬币又不尽相同。比如在美国，便士，尤其是正面朝上的便士代表幸运；在英国，六便士硬币代表幸运。

有些动物专门与运气或祈盼好运密切相关。金鱼是繁荣、财富、智慧、力量、长寿与和平的象征。海豚是幸运和守护的象征。这是因为古代水手相信当船靠近陆地时，他们会在船的周围看到海豚。兔子被认为是幸运的，因为它们与万物生长的春天相关，兔脚可以作为一种幸运符佩戴或携带。蝴蝶是

ships when they neared land. Rabbits are considered lucky since they are associated with spring, the season of new life, and a rabbit's foot can be worn or carried as a lucky charm. A butterfly is a symbol of freedom and perfection in nature. Many people have found through personal experience that butterflies are omens of good luck.

There are even a few foods that can be used to wish for good luck. Black-eyed peas are eaten in the southern United States in the New Year for good luck. Lentils look similar to coins and are thus eaten for good fortune in parts of Italy. Fish is considered lucky food in parts of North America, Asia, and Europe since fish "swim forward" toward new goals. They also swim in large schools, so they represent abundance.

Some gestures, while not exactly wishing for good luck, try to ward off misfortune. These are called "avoidant actions", and some people think they are effective ways to ensure neutral or good luck. If you hear a British person say "touch wood" or "knock on wood", you'll probably see him/her touch, tap,

大自然中自由和完美的象征。许多人通过亲身经历发现蝴蝶是好运的兆头。

甚至有些食物也可以用来祈盼好运。在美国南部，人们在新年食用豇豆以求好运。在意大利的部分地区，人们吃小扁豆来祈盼好运，这是因为它们看起来与硬币相似。在北美、亚洲和欧洲的部分地区，人们认为吃鱼能带来好运，因为鱼总是游向新目标，而且它们还成群结队地游，所以鱼象征着富足。

有些手势尽管并不完全是为了祈盼好运，但却意在避免不幸。这些手势被称为"回避动作"。有些人认为它们是祈盼好运或确保至少平安无事的有效方法。如果你听到英国人说要"触摸木头"或"敲打木头"，你可能会看到他们真的在触摸或敲打木制品。英国人试图用这种

or knock something that is made from wood at the same time. British people do this when they are trying to send away bad luck.

Every culture and country has a different symbol or practice that they believe will bring them luck. As cultures have evolved and assimilated, these good luck methods have been spread in different parts of the world.

方法来驱散厄运。

每种文化和每个国家都有不同的代表好运的象征和祈盼好运的方法。随着文化的发展和融合，这些祈盼好运的方法已经在世界各地传播开来。

练习二

中国文化中的吉祥寓意

中国文化中有很多寓意吉祥的表达，其中大多从古代沿用至今，并仍然在人们的日常生活中发挥着重要作用。让我们从幸运色、动物、双关语和数字这四个方面来探讨中华文化的独特魅力。

颜色在中国文化中很重要，因为它们富有寓意。在人们的日常生活以及一些特殊场合中，红色、黄色和绿色被认为是三种主要的幸运色。以红色为例，每一个中国人都知道红色象征着一切美好的事物。在古代王室看来，它代表权力、地

Expressions to Wish for Good Luck in Chinese Culture

There are many expressions to wish for good luck in Chinese culture. They are mostly derived from ancient times and still take on an important role in people's daily lives today. Let's explore the unique charm of Chinese culture from lucky colors, animals, puns, and numbers.

Colors are important in Chinese culture as they are endowed with meanings. The three main colors considered lucky in people's daily lives as well as on special occasions are red, yellow, and green. Take red for example. Every Chinese knows that red symbolizes all

位以及威信；普通老百姓则视它为幸福、富足以及好运气的象征。红色被广泛应用于节日和婚礼等重要活动中。例如，传统的中式结婚礼服和装饰都是红色的，并且观礼的客人会给新婚夫妇红包。

中国神话故事中流传的各种神兽，比如龙、麒麟和凤凰等，在中国传统文化中占有重要的地位，可以说它们是中华文明的象征。虽然它们都是虚构的动物，但它们的形象和价值对中国人来说意义深远。例如，龙代表无上尊贵、力量、富饶和祥瑞。古代帝王被认为是龙子，中国人则把自己看作是龙的传人。

采用谐音寓意吉祥的方法在中国广为流行，并已经逐渐成为中国

good things. It represents power, status, and authority to ancient Chinese royalty, while to ordinary people, red means happiness, wealth, prosperity, and good luck. Red is widely used for important events like festivals and weddings. For example, the traditional Chinese wedding dress and decorations are all in red, and the guests invited to the wedding would give out red envelopes to the newlyweds.

The various beasts circulated in Chinese mythology, such as dragons, unicorns, and phoenixes, occupy an important position in traditional Chinese culture and can be considered as a symbol of the Chinese civilization. Although they are all imaginary creatures, their image and value have far-reaching significance for the Chinese. For example, dragons represent the greatest royalty, strength, prosperity, and auspiciousness. The ancient emperors of China were identified as the sons of dragons, and the Chinese people see themselves as descendants of dragons.

A popular method of seeking good fortune in China is using homonyms

文化的重要组成部分。中文里有数不清的有趣的同音异义字，中国人在日常生活中喜爱使用双关语，尤其喜欢采用有吉祥寓意的谐音字作为幸运词。例如，"鸡"和"鱼"的谐音含义分别是"吉祥"和"富余"，这就是为什么在新年盛宴上肯定会有鸡肉和鱼肉的菜肴。

在中国文化中，有些数字是幸运数，因为它们的发音与幸运词的发音相似。让我们以"六""八"和"九"为例。"六"听起来像"流"，因此祝福语"六六大顺"的意思是"一切都顺顺利利"。"八"与"发"同韵，后者意味着繁荣和财富。"九"和"长长久久"的发音类似，意思是"永远、永恒和长寿"。幸运数在中国文化中非常重要。人们在挑选住所、电话号码、营业地址以及结婚、节日和其他庆祝活动日期时都会选择幸运数。

with their auspicious meanings, which has gradually become an important part of the Chinese culture. In Chinese language, there are loads of interesting homophonic words, and the Chinese people love to use puns in their daily lives, particularly using those homonyms implying auspiciousness as their lucky words. For example, chicken and fish in Chinese are pronounced as "jī" and "yú" with their homonyms as "lucky" and "abundance" respectively, and this is why there are certainly chicken and fish dishes in the New Year feast.

In Chinese culture, certain numbers are considered lucky, because their pronunciations sound similar to words with lucky meanings. Let's take six, eight, and nine as examples. The Chinese pronunciation of six (六/liù) sounds like flow (流/liú), so the blessing phrase "六六大顺" (liùliù dàshùn) means "everything flows smoothly". Eight (八/bā) in Chinese rhymes with "fā" (发), which means prosperity and wealth. Nine (九/jiǔ) in Chinese has a similar-sounding phrase: "长长久久" (chángcháng jiǔjiǔ), which means "forever, ever-lasting, and longevity".

中文中幸运色、动物、双关语和数字的用法都非常独特和有趣，这让中国文化更具魅力。

Lucky numbers are very important in Chinese culture. People select lucky numbers when choosing residences, telephone numbers, business addresses, and dates of weddings, festivals, and other celebratory events.

The usage of lucky colors, animals, puns, and numbers in Chinese language is quite unique and interesting, which makes the Chinese culture more charming.

2.3.2 口译的非语言知识

口译的非语言知识可以概括为三个方面：百科知识、专业知识和情景知识。

1. 百科知识

在口译实践中，译员会遇到不同的讲话人和各种交际场合，话题千变万化，内容包罗万象。钟述孔（2001）认为译员应对一切都有所了解，拥有"百科全书般的知识"。这种百科知识可以包括多个方面，如中外政治、经贸、文化、科技、历史、地理、语言、文学、艺术、医学、法律、宗教和民俗（包括民族、社会、风俗、家庭及衣食住行），等等。

例如，对于"Marriage is between Adam and Eve, not Adam and Steve, nor Madam and Eve."，译员需要了解 Adam and Eve（亚当和夏娃）出自《圣经》，意指"男女结合，组成婚姻家庭"；Steve 是西方很常见的男性名字，用在这里同 Eve 押韵，与 Adam 同指男性，Madam 和 Eve 同指女性，意指"同性婚姻"。所以，这句话应理解为"婚姻应是异性而非同性之间的结合"。

又如，对于"He claims the Catholic faith. Yet the Vatican is no fan of his science."（他自称为天主教徒，然而天主教会并不支持他的研究），译员只有知道

Vatican（梵蒂冈）是天主教的中心，即它代表什么，才能对这句话有所理解。

由于中国与西方国家在地理环境、生活习惯、宗教信仰、历史和文学典故等方面存在差异，两者语言内涵不同，词语表达也有所区别。

1）地理环境差异（Difference in Geography）

语言根植于自然地理环境中。英国是一个岛国，四面环海，渔业和航海业是其经济中的两个重要组成部分；中国人的生活则与土地息息相关。因此，有些英汉语言内涵虽然相同，但表达方式却不同。例如：

- 挥金如土

  spend money like water

- 力大如牛

  as strong as a horse

- 奋力图存

  to keep one's head above water

- 殊途同归

  All roads lead to Rome.

- 这山望着那山高

  The grass is always greener on the other side of the fence.

2）生活习惯差异（Difference in Living Habits）

因为生活环境不同，人们的生活习惯也不同，这些不同会体现在语言中。例如：

- 过着牛马不如的生活

  to lead a dog life

- 瘦得像猴

  as thin as a shadow

- 水底捞月

  fish in the air

- 他是个叛徒。

  He was a cat in the pan.

- 那是小菜一碟。

  That's a piece of cake.

又如，英国人的主食是面包，中国人的主食是米饭，所以汉语中有"饭碗""夹生饭""鱼米之乡""生米煮成熟饭""巧妇难为无米之炊"等表达；英语中有"Don't quarrel with your bread and butter.""Half a loaf is better than none."和 earn one's bread 这种表达。

3）宗教信仰差异（Difference in Religion and Belief）

佛教自一千多年前传入中国后，经过发展逐渐融入中国各个社会领域。所以，汉语中有很多与佛相关的表达方式，如"借花献佛""临时抱佛脚""跑了和尚，跑不了庙""菩萨心肠""放下屠刀立地成佛"等。基督教深深根植于西方人的生活中。因此，大量的英语表达源于《圣经》或与教会有关，如"God helps those who help themselves.""Man proposes, God disposes."和 as poor as the church mouse 等。

4）历史和文学典故差异（Difference in Historical and Literary Allusions）

典故是历史、传说、寓言、文学或宗教中的人物或事件。因为它们深深根植于语言中，所以几乎所有人在说话时或多或少都会引用一些。汉语中有很多表达来自中国的四大古典名著。例如：

- 林黛玉式的人物（《红楼梦》）

  Lin Daiyu-style characters (to be always melancholy and over sensitive) (*A Dream of Red Mansions*)

- 说曹操，曹操就到。（《三国演义》）

  Talk of Caocao, and he is sure to come. / Talk of the devil and he's sure to appear. (*Romance of the Three Kingdoms*)

- 逼上梁山（《水浒传》）

  to be forced to join the Liangshan Rebels / be forced to do something (*Water Margin*)

- 猪八戒吃人参果，全不知滋味。（《西游记》）

  Pig Bajie who eats ginseng fruit has no time to taste it. / gobble up something without enjoying the taste (*Journey to the West*)

英语中有许多表达来自《圣经》、古希腊和古罗马神话以及莎士比亚的文学宝库。例如：

- Hercules' task (extremely difficult task)

  赫拉克勒斯的任务，喻指艰巨的任务。（古希腊神话）

- a Pandora's box

  潘多拉魔盒，喻指一切灾祸之源。（古希腊神话）

- the Achilles' heel (the only fatal weakness) (*The Iliad*)

  阿喀琉斯之踵，喻指致命的弱点、要害。（荷马史诗《伊利亚特》）

- It's all Greek to me (I don't know anything about it). (*Julius Caesar*)

  我对此一窍不通。（莎士比亚《尤利乌斯·恺撒》）

- To be, or not to be; it's a question. (*Hamlet*)

  生存还是毁灭，这是个问题。（莎士比亚《哈姆雷特》）

2. 专业知识

译员除了具备口译的通用知识外，还应积累相关领域的专业知识。各个行业都有自己的行话和专门术语，对这些知识的掌握与否会直接影响口译的效果。例如，科技口译可以包括国际学术会议、科技报告会、讲座、培训班、展览会、新产品发布会、引进设备技术谈判等方面；商务口译不再局限于以往的进出口、业务谈判、函电等，而是涵盖贸易、金融、经济、商法、营销等多方面。随着社会的快速发展和科技的进步，更多新的领域、新的专业会不断地涌现。因此，译员平时不但要注意专业知识的积累，在进行某次专业口译任务之前，还需进行必要的准备。

首先，译员需要掌握基本的专业知识，这需要大量地阅读相关的资料、文章和书籍，必要时还需要向有关专家请教。尽管译员不必成为这方面的专家，但相关领域的知识不可或缺。其次，译员需要大量地搜集并强化记忆相关的英汉对照专业术语。有些术语虽和常用词汇是同一词，但词义却大相径庭。例如，在商务英语中，more or less 是"溢短装"的意思，documentation 是"制单"的意思；在保险领域，open policy 或 open cover 是"预约保险"的意思，general average 是"共同海损"的意思，等等。此外，有些术语是某个专业独有的词汇，并不常见，也不常用，译员需要重点掌握。译员如果对某一专业或主题比较熟悉，对术语运用较为自如，那么在口译时自然就可以摆脱源语的束缚，更准确地传递信息。

3. 情景知识

口译的情景知识包括交际的时间、地点、主题，交际的正式程度和交际参与者的相互关系等。译员在进行口译前，应尽可能地了解和掌握讲话人和听众的情况，工作环境以及谈话内容等。例如事先了解讲话人的基本情况是非常有必要的，如教育、职业和文化背景，社会环境，使用语言，主要观点和看法，以及讲话人与听众的关系等。译员对讲话人、话题、体裁和语境越熟悉，就越在认知层面上接近演讲者，就越容易理解说话人的意思，从而口译的准确度就越高。

Gilles（2013：43—46）也强调，在口译过程中，语言知识和非语言知识"相互重叠和交织"，理解语言就是理解其蕴含的知识。他列出一系列增加背景知识、提高外语水平的方法，如广泛阅读各种报纸、杂志（包括专业杂志）和书籍；充分利用网络查询，如维基百科，既要了解某个词语的意思，也要了解其背景及相关知识；使用双语词典查找词的含义；听广播、看电视或网上收看新闻访谈节目、电影、电视剧等，特别是观看英语母语使用者经常看的节目；欣赏流行歌曲、记歌词等；把电脑及软件的使用语言设置为外语；整理各种专题的报纸文件档案，进行两种语言的对比，等等。

> 课后作业：专门建一个文件夹，按照专题进行分类、收集和整理自己每日阅读报纸、期刊、图书或网络资料等时所学到的背景知识。

2.4 口译听辨与逻辑分析

口译的听与理解是一个包含听取信息、理解会意和逻辑分析在内的快速而复杂的过程。这一过程可以分为以下五个层次：

- 迅速对源语内容要点进行标定并做出整理，把握语篇整体意义。
- 抓住要点之间的逻辑关系。
- 将话语的主题、语境、交际环境、语言的前后句法关系、各种副语言信息和其他语言外的"认知库"信息纳入理解轨道。
- 利用译前准备或译员预先储存、积累的口译经验为口译现场理解提供一定的参照值。
- 迅速地、半自动化地进行译语搜觅并对关键词语、数字或术语等做出代码转换。

（鲍刚，2005：114）

口译的逻辑分析是指在听与理解的过程中，译员对话语进行纵向和横向的分析。纵向分析是指分清关键信息和辅助信息，即找出话语的逻辑层次；横向分析是指明确各信息点之间的逻辑关系。一般信息都遵从一定的逻辑关系模式，或归纳推理，或溯因推理，或演绎推理，如概括（generalization）、分类（classification）、因果（cause-effect）和对比对照（compare and contrast），按照时间、空间、步骤或重要性的顺序排列信息等。通过对信息的点（主要信息）、线（各要点之间的联系)和面(细节信息)进行全面的梳理整合,译员可以透彻地理解话语的内容。

2.4.1 口译思路归纳分析

口译的话语语类大致可以分为四种:叙述语类、介绍语类、论证语类和对话语类。每一类话语都拥有自己的常规话语结构和相对固定的篇章推理及加工模式,表现为反复使用的、雷同度很高的语段结构。译员可以利用不同语体的材料进行口译思路归纳训练,运用分析与综合、分类与比较、归纳与演绎、抽象与概括等逻辑方法找出篇章的主体结构,从而形成良好的逻辑思维习惯,提高自身的逻辑整理能力和信息整合能力。

口译思路归纳分析的目的是归纳不同话语的常用结构,并结合背景知识预测讲话内容的主体结构,总结讲话人的目的、内容和结论。具体操作时可以选用条理清楚、层次分明、言语难度适中的书面演讲稿,如叙述类、论证类和介绍类的演讲稿,并在规定时间内完成以下训练内容:一是圈出要点,标出表示因果、转折等逻辑关系的标志词,并归纳出讲话人的思路;二是口头概述演讲稿,要求重点层次分明、逻辑关系清楚。

1. 叙述语类

叙述语类有两个特点:一是叙述的话语结构与叙述的时间顺序紧密相关;二是叙述过程中插入的描绘总是遵循多数人能接受的空间线索,以构成某种特定的画面。这类话语结构常用于典故、故事和笑话等。叙述语类的时间结构如下所示:

引子——时间
　　——地点(+描绘、悬念、叙事铺垫等)
　　——人物

情节发展——发展1（＋描绘、悬念、叙事铺垫等）

　　　　——发展2（＋描绘、悬念、叙事铺垫等）

　　　　——发展N（＋描绘、悬念、叙事铺垫或"包袱"铺垫等）

高潮或"包袱"

结尾

（鲍刚，2005：43—46）

> 技巧训练：阅读下列故事，找出故事的结构线索，并用汉语复述故事梗概。

练习三

孙悟空三打白骨精

唐僧与徒弟孙悟空、猪八戒和沙僧去西天取经，一路历尽磨难。幸亏悟空火眼金睛，善识妖怪，除恶降魔，保得师父平安无事。

这一天，师徒四人行至崇山峻岭之间，又饥又渴。悟空用金箍棒在地上画了一个圆圈，让师父坐在里面休息，以防妖怪近身。自己则跳上云端，寻找食物。

在山中修炼千年的白骨精，一直注视着唐僧的行踪。她听说若食唐僧之肉，将会长生不老，便设法靠近。她趁悟空不在，变成一个少女，面如桃花，眉似柳叶，手提一只盛满食物的瓷罐，笑盈盈地向唐僧等人走来。贪吃好色的八戒，顾不得许多，忙跳出圆圈，招呼师父上前搭话。少女走近唐僧，正要叙话。恰巧悟空摘桃回来，认出白骨精的嘴脸，他大喝一声，当头一棒，吓得白骨精化作一缕轻烟逃走，留下一具少女假尸。唐僧不识真相，埋怨悟空不该杀人，悟空指着瓷罐中的蛆虫、癞蛤蟆，提醒师父不要上当，唐僧半信半疑。

白骨精逃回洞中，咬牙切齿，不肯罢休。她再次变成一位满脸皱纹的老太婆，向唐僧讨要自己的女儿。仁慈的唐僧哪里知道妖怪的诡计，一时不知如何应对。悟空知道白骨精又在耍花招，二话不说，举棒便打。白骨精再次化作轻烟飞去，留下一具假尸在地。唐僧十分生气，训斥悟空随便伤人，口念咒语，使悟空头上的金箍越勒越紧，疼得悟空满地打滚。

　　白骨精为了离间唐僧师徒，又变作一位白发苍苍的老公公，悟空见是妖精刚要动手，唐僧急忙上前拦阻。悟空不顾一切，抡棒打下，白骨精如法炮制，留下假尸，欺骗唐僧。唐僧不辨真相，不能原谅悟空，把他赶回花果山。

　　白骨精见悟空离去，便肆无忌惮，率众妖把唐僧等人捉进洞中。八戒奋力逃出洞外，直奔花果山请回悟空。悟空扮成白骨精之母，进洞救下师父、沙僧。为制服妖精，悟空摇身一变，在白骨精面前幻化出成千上万个替身，使她不能动弹。一把大火，烧得白骨精原形毕露，变成一堆白骨。唐僧见状恍然大悟，知道错怪了悟空。师徒一行继续西行。

练习四

Rapunzel

A long time ago, a man and his wife were expecting their first baby. As time passed, the wife spent much of her day resting. She would stare out of the window into a beautiful garden filled with wonderful flowers and herbs. No one ever dared to enter this garden because it was owned by a horrible witch.

One day, as the wife was looking into the garden, she noticed a clump of a delicious-looking herb. It was called rapunzel, and it looked so fresh and sweet that she could almost taste it.

In the days that followed, the woman spent more and more of her time gazing at the rapunzel. Before long, she grew quite miserable.

"What's wrong, my dear?" asked her husband.

"I want to eat the rapunzel in the witch's garden," she replied. "I think I'll be ill if I don't have some soon."

The man couldn't bear to see his wife suffer, so that night he tiptoed into the witch's garden, grabbed a bunch of rapunzel and ran back home.

His wife was overjoyed. The rapunzel tasted so delicious that she wanted more. So the next night, her husband once again tiptoed into the witch's garden.

He was just about to pick the rapunzel when an ugly-looking figure jumped out at him. It was the wicked witch.

"Caught you, you thieving toad," she cackled. "You'll regret ever sneaking in here and stealing my rapunzel."

"Forgive me!" cried the man. "My wife is expecting a baby. She told me she would fall ill if she couldn't eat some of your delicious rapunzel."

"A baby, eh?" grinned the toothless witch. "Hmm! You may take as much rapunzel as you like, but you must give me your baby once it is born. If you don't agree, I will turn you and your wife into toads."

The man had no choice, so he quickly agreed.

Shortly after, the woman gave birth to a beautiful baby girl. The parents were overjoyed, but their happiness was short lived. As soon as they wondered what to name her, the wicked witch appeared. "She shall be called Rapunzel," cackled the witch. Then she took the baby and disappeared.

Rapunzel grew into a very pretty girl, with beautiful, long golden hair.

When she was sixteen years old, the witch locked her in a room at the top of a very tall tower. The tower had no door or stairs. The only way in was through a single window.

Every day the witch came and stood at the bottom of the tower, and called, "Rapunzel, Rapunzel, let down your fair hair."

Rapunzel would then lower her long hair through the window, and the witch would use it as a ladder.

One day, a handsome prince was riding in the woods when he heard Rapunzel singing. The prince followed the beautiful sound until he came to the tower. But, finding there was no way in, he went away. However, he was so enchanted with Rapunzel's voice that he returned to listen to her day after day.

One day, as the prince was hiding in the trees, he saw the witch arrive and call out, "Rapunzel, Rapunzel, let down your fair hair."

Then he watched in amazement as Rapunzel's golden hair tumbled to the ground and the witch climbed up into the tower. The prince waited until the witch had gone and then he went to the tower.

"Rapunzel, Rapunzel, let down your fair hair." He cried.

At once Rapunzel's hair fell to the ground and up climbed the prince. Rapunzel was afraid when she saw the prince, but his kind words soon calmed her. "I heard your beautiful voice," he explained. "Now that I've seen you, I will not rest until you agree to marry me."

Rapunzel was quite in love with the handsome prince and quickly agreed. "First, I must escape though. Bring me some silk and I will weave a ladder. Then I will be able to climb down."

So each day, after the witch had left, the prince came with silk.

The witch suspected nothing until one day Rapunzel said to the witch, "You are so much heavier than the prince." As soon as she had said these words, Rapunzel knew she was in trouble.

"You wicked girl," screeched the witch. She grabbed a pair of scissors and cut off Rapunzel's long hair. Then she cast a spell whisking Rapunzel away to a far-off place.

That night, when the prince came to the tower, the witch was ready.

"Rapunzel, Rapunzel, let down your fair hair," called the prince. Holding on tight, the witch let Rapunzel's hair fall to the ground and up climbed the prince.

"Ha!" cried the witch. "Rapunzel's gone and you'll never set eyes on her again." Then she let go of Rapunzel's lovely locks and the prince fell to the ground. Unluckily, some rose thorns pricked his eyes and blinded him.

In the years that followed, the blind prince looked everywhere for his lost love. One day, he heard the same sweet voice he had heard before. As he wandered towards it, Rapunzel saw her handsome prince again. She ran to him weeping. The prince gathered her into his arms and her tears fell into his eyes. At once he could see again.

The prince took Rapunzel back to his kingdom, where they married and lived happily ever after.

2. 介绍语类

介绍语类常用于对物品、人物、旅游景点、企业、团体等的介绍。其言语结构特点符合人们对一般事物的认知规律：一是正式介绍前存在某种"引言"语段，有时介绍者可以在这一语段内采用某些修辞手法，以吸引听者的注意；二是介绍时一般由表及里、由浅入深，基本上符合多数人的思维路线，而且"主线"介绍有时会遵循一定的空间或时间线索；三是介绍多具有层次感，表现出一定的逻辑顺序；四是语篇结束时一般有一处小结。（鲍刚，2005：46—48）

> 技巧训练：阅读下列短文，圈出要点和逻辑关系词，并用源语归纳大意。

练习五

互联网发展

近年来，随着互联网技术的快速发展和演变，我国互联网发展呈现出四个方面的新变化。一是在信息形态方面，信息传播形式以文字为主向音频、视频、图片等多媒体形态转变。目前，我国网上音视频等多媒体信息占互联网流量的50%以上，这极大丰富了网上信息的表现形式，同时也加大了信息内容安全监管的难度。二是在应用领域方面，我国互联网正从以信息传播和娱乐消费为主向商务服务领域延伸，互联网开始逐步深入到国民经济更深层次和更宽领域。这对于优化我国互联网消费结构、促进经济发展模式转变具有积极意义，同时也对网络诚信建设提出了更高要求。三是在服务模式方面，互联网正从提供信息服务向提供平台服务延伸。以博客、播客为代表的 Web 2.0 服务模式使互联网的平台功能更加突出，网民不仅是信息的消费者，也是信息的提供者、创造者。这大大丰富了网上的信息内容，同时也对网民的守法自律提出了更高要求。四是在传播手段方面，传统互联网正在向移动互联网延伸，手机上网成为新潮流。基于移动互联网的新媒体形态不断出现，移动互联网市场规模不断扩大，这大大拓宽了网络信息的传播渠道，同时也对规范网络信息传播秩序提出了更高要求。

练习六

Education Revolutions

The history of education is the history of humanity. Only three education revolutions can be said to have occurred during the last three to five million years. The beginnings of learning from others, in family units, groups, and tribes, constitute the first education revolution. Learning was being handed down from generation to generation with knowledge about how to use the tools, how to hunt, how to build seasonal camps, how to use fire, and how to migrate over long distances. The second phase of institutionalized education was altered in following the end of the last Ice Age in 10000 B.C. Now we can see the origins of settled life. Villages, followed by towns and cities, began to appear. These new societies demanded a new range of specialism, including knowledge about agriculture, trade, law, civic society, technology, and religion. Schools and universities had emerged, but the education remained for the privileged few. The third education revolution began 500 years ago. With the development of printing, text books began to be widely produced for the first time, which transformed learning and education for the masses. However, for all the impact of new technology and digitization during the last 50 years, the task of teaching and the classroom/lecture hall remains fundamentally the same as it was in

1600. The next, evolving artificial intelligence (AI), alongside augmented reality (AR) and virtual reality (VR), will be the fourth education revolution. AI is an altogether new way of spreading education across the world.

3. 论证语类

论证语类与介绍语类在结构上有很多相似的特点，如都有引言，都有层次感，都有结论等，但是论证语类的逻辑性更强，并且有"论点+论据"这种介绍语类没有的结构特点。这类话语结构清晰，转折明确，逻辑严谨，特别适用于逻辑归纳记忆法。论证语类的层次结构如下所示：

引言

论点 1 —— 论据 a

　　　　　论据 b

　　　　　……

　　　　　论据 N + 小结

论点 2 —— 论据 a

　　　　　论据 b

　　　　　……

　　　　　论据 N + 小结

论点 N　　论据 a

　　　　　论据 b

　　　　　……

　　　　　论据 N + 小结

结论

> 技巧训练：阅读下列演讲稿，用口译思路归纳分析方法概述其要点、思路。

练习七

 背景知识

"中英数学教师交流项目"是中英高级别人文交流机制的重要成果之一。2014年,在北京举行的中英高级别人文交流机制第二次会议上,上海市教委和英国教育部签订备忘录,开启了"中英数学教师交流项目"。鉴于2014年至2018年四期项目取得的丰硕成果以及积极的社会影响,双方决定继续开展两轮新项目,一直持续到2020年。在前两轮的合作中,以小学数学教师交流为主,后期双方的合作全面进入中学阶段领域。英国教育部教育标准司司长保尔·凯特表示,"中英数学教师交流项目"成功地做到了互利共赢,也为进一步深化中英数学教学合作创造了更多的可行性。

为中英教育交流合作增光添彩[1]

尊敬的英国教育国务大臣吉布阁下,

尊敬的各位校长、各位老师,

女士们、先生们、朋友们,

大家晚上好!

欢迎大家作客中国大使馆!很高兴在中国传统佳节来临之际,与中英教育界朋友们欢聚一堂,共叙友情,共迎新春。我谨对长期支持两国教育交流合作的各界人士,特别是参与"中英数学教师交流项目"的各位校长、各位老师表示衷心感谢!

教育是立国之本、兴国之基。教育交流与合作是中英关系的重要组成部分,也奠定了两国关系的民意根基。我对此高度重视,倾注了大量时间和精力,使馆同事们称我为"爱教大使",我对这一头衔感到骄傲。对于"中英数学教师交流项目",我认为有三方面重要意义:

---

[1] 2019年1月25日,中国驻英国大使馆刘晓明大使在"中英数学教师交流项目"新年招待会上的讲话。来自中国驻英国大使馆网站。

首先，这是促交流、拓合作的品牌项目。近年来，中英教育合作内涵日益丰富，涵盖了从学龄前教育、基础教育到职业教育、高等教育、语言文化交流等广泛领域。"中英数学教师交流项目"应运而生。在短短4年时间里，该项目一路走来，从无到有，从小到大，现在已经成为两国教育合作的一大亮点。双方迄已互派5批中小学教师720多人次，有力推动两国教育交流合作走深走实。

第二，这是打基础、利长远的互惠平台。数学是十分重要的基础学科，有"学科之母"的美誉。在本次"中英数学教师交流项目"中，分别有86位上海中小学数学教师来英、90多位英国数学老师前往上海交流。项目紧扣提高教师教学能力的主题，设计了形式灵活、内容丰富的学习研修模式。两国中小学数学老师深入交流、相互学习、切磋技能，直接惠及中英数百所学校及数万名学生，产生广泛积极影响，为提升两国基础教育水平注入新动力。

第三，这是增互鉴、促了解的有益实践。文明交流互鉴是不可阻挡的历史潮流，是推动人类文明进步和世界和平发展的重要动力。中国和英国是东西方文明的代表性国家。"中英数学教师交流项目"是中国与西方发达国家开展的首个大规模教师交流项目，对促进东西方文明交流互鉴具有重要意义。我相信，参与该项目的师生在教学和学习的过程中，都能亲身体验彼此文化，增进互学互鉴，促进了解友谊。

中国人常说，"百年大计，教育为本""教育大计，教师为本"。这对于教育及教师来说，既是一种重视与肯定，也是一份责任与使命。借此机会，我想就"中英数学教师交流项目"未来发展提两点希望：

一是相互学习，共同提高。中英数学教学的理念和方法各有所长。英国作为世界上最早建立现代教育体系的国家，诞生了牛顿、图灵等伟大数学家。中国古代也产生了刘徽、祖冲之等伟大数学家，他们对人类科学的贡献，至今仍为我们享用。中英两国教师通过数学项目合作可以相互学习，互通有无，取长补短，共同提高。

二是教书育人，传承友谊。国之交在于民相亲，民相亲在于心相知。

中英历史文化、社会制度不同，发展阶段各异，加强交流与沟通尤显重要。今年是中英建立代办级外交关系65周年，中英关系历经沧桑，不断发展，很大程度上得益于两国人民之间的密切交往和深厚友谊。青年是国家的未来，也是中英关系的未来。我希望各位老师在传授数学知识的同时，也将友好的种子播种在青年学生的心田，使中英友谊世代相传。

再过9天就是中国农历新年——"猪年"。猪在中国文化中象征着财富和吉祥。我希望并相信，新的一年，在双方共同努力下，"中英数学教师交流项目"一定会不断开拓创新、开花结果，为中英教育交流合作增光添彩！

最后，我提议，

为中英关系"黄金时代"行稳致远，

为中英教育合作不断发展，

为在座的各位朋友猪年吉祥、万事如意，

干杯！

练习八

The Importance of Studying Abroad[1]

We believe that relationships between nations aren't just about relationships between governments or leaders—they're about relationships between people, particularly young people. So, we view study abroad programs not just as an educational opportunity for students, but also as a vital part of a country's foreign policy.

Through the wonders of modern technology, our world is more connected than ever before. Ideas can cross oceans with the click of a button. Companies can do business and compete with companies across the globe. And we can text, e-mail, and Skype with people on every continent.

1　Extracts from Remarks by the First Lady at Stanford Center at Peking University on March 22, 2014. From The White House Office of the First Lady website.

So, studying abroad isn't just a fun way to spend a semester; it is quickly becoming the key to success in our global economy. Because getting ahead in today's workplaces isn't just about getting good grades or test scores in school, which are important. It's also about having real experience with the world beyond your borders—experience with languages, cultures, and societies very different from your own. Or, as the Chinese saying goes: "It is better to travel ten thousand miles than to read ten thousand books."

But let's be clear, studying abroad is about so much more than improving your own future. It's also about shaping the future of your countries and of the world we all share. Because when it comes to the defining challenges of our time—whether it's climate change or economic opportunity or the spread of nuclear weapons—these are shared challenges. And no one country can confront them alone. The only way forward is together.

That's why it is so important for young people like you to live and study in each other's countries, because that's how you develop that habit of cooperation. You do it by immersing yourself in one another's culture, by learning each other's stories, and by getting past the stereotypes and misconceptions that too often divide us.

That's how you come to understand how much we all share. That's how you realize that we all have a stake in each other's success—that cures discovered here in Beijing could save lives in America, that clean energy technologies from Silicon Valley in California could improve the environment here in China, and that the architecture of an ancient temple in Xi'an could inspire the design of new buildings in Dallas or Detroit.

These lasting bonds represent the true value of studying abroad. And I am thrilled that more and more students are getting this opportunity.

4. 对话语类

对话语类逻辑性差，结构松散，十分接近日常生活中使用的口语，多见于寒暄、问候、交谈、聚会等主宾较随意的对话中。对话看似随意，没有规律可循，但若要保证言语交际的顺利进行，交际双方必须遵循一定的会话原则，即合作原则。哲学家 Grice（1975）提出"合作原则"（principles of cooperation），认为人们的言语交际是互相合作的，谈话双方都希望能互相理解、共同配合。因此，说话人和听话人之间必然遵循着某种默契来促成合作，如数量准则（quantity maxim），即说的话应包含言谈所需的信息，不应超出所需的信息；质量准则（quality maxim），即不说自知是不真实的话，或缺乏足够证据的话；关联准则（relevant maxim），即说的话必然与所谈内容有关；方式准则（manner maxim），即说话要清楚、有条理，避免晦涩、歧义、啰唆。

借用亚里士多德的联想法则，对话语类的逻辑线索可以呈现出三种规律，即接近律、类似律和对比律。接近律是指在时间或空间上接近的事物容易发生联想（如河与船）；类似律则是指在形貌或内涵上相似的事物容易发生联想（如用绿色比拟生命）；对比律是指在性质或特点上相反的事物容易发生联想（如黑与白）。（亚里士多德，1992）

在对话口译中，如果译员能够注意双方谈话的上下文逻辑关联和规律，跟上谈话的思路和节奏，就能更顺利地完成口译任务。

> 小组练习：三人一组，分别担任中文、英文对话者和口译员，进行交替口译练习。

练习九

A：您一定是罗斯教授了。您好！

B: Yes, it's me. Nice to meet you!

A：很高兴见到您。

B: This is my book for you.

A：谢谢！这是给您的中国风景台历，还有一盒中国著名的正山小种武夷红茶。今年年初梅首相访华时，习近平主席就是用正山小种茶招待她的。

B: Thank you. It is such an honor.

A: 听说您之前生病了。很高兴您已康复。

B: I had bad health in the summer. Now, I have recovered my health. I worked too hard. Perhaps I should slow down.

A: 您在授课和科研上如何分配自己的时间呢?

A: I have a heavy load of teaching tasks, taking more than 50% of my time. I usually teach a half day for the first month in each term. And the rest two months, I teach less and spend more time on my research. The more I do research, the wider sphere I involved myself. I sometimes stay up late till 1 a.m.

B: 读书也是如此。读的书越多,越觉得时间不够用。但我们还是要平衡我们的工作、生活和健康。

C: I totally agree with you.

A: 感谢您拨冗和我们见面,并邀请我们共进午餐。按照我们事先商定好的,我希望了解您对经济全球化的看法。

B: Thank you for consulting me. It is my pleasure to host you for lunch and share my thoughts with you.

2.4.2 口译听辨理解分析

口译的听辨理解不只是单纯听语言的外在形式,而是理解所听到的内容意义,即脱离源语语言外壳的意义。这需要译员在听的同时进行预测、分析、判断和推理,通过听辨理解分析,掌握叙述、论证、介绍等语类语篇的逻辑结构,进而增强预测和逻辑推理能力。

听辨理解分析练习是进行无笔记听和理解短文,即听完后要先说出短文的中心大意、内容要点以及逻辑关联,最后再复述出来。练习的重点应该放在技巧的掌握上,而不是单纯的语言听力上。这样可以节约对源语进行分析和整合的时间,更合理地分配注意力,达到更好的理解效果。

第二章 口译听辨理解与逻辑分析

> 技巧训练：听下列录音，进行口译听辨理解分析训练。要求不记笔记，并用汉语复述原文。

练习十 中英是"一带一路"的"天然合作伙伴"

练习十一 中国的消费能力和消费需求大幅提升

练习十二 Trade and Economic Relations Between China and the U.S.

练习十三 China's Achievements in 40 Years of Reform and Opening-up

第三章 口译的短期记忆

记忆是一个对信息编码、储存和提取的过程,可以分为短期记忆和长期记忆。短期记忆是一种有限的容量储存,可以保持信息大约20~30秒;长期记忆是一个学习、获取知识的过程,储存在长期记忆中的信息可以保持相当长一段时间,能持续数周、数月,甚至一生。记忆是口译过程中的关键环节之一,译员主要依靠其长期记忆来理解源语信息,依靠其短期记忆对所听内容进行回忆和再表达。

在口译过程中,源语信息可谓转瞬即逝,译员需要在有限的时间内最大限度地发挥其记忆力,储存和回忆所听内容,从而进行代码转换。不但记忆强度大,而且准确度要求高。这种记忆并不仅仅是对所接收信息的简单储存,而是对该信息进行主动加工、整合后的记录、保存和提取。只有采取合理的记忆方法来减少记忆的负荷,才能准确、有效地储存信息。

口译中的记忆训练主要是指短期记忆训练,它包括视觉化记忆训练、概括性记忆训练和篇章结构程式化记忆训练等。通过系统、科学的记忆训练,译员可以增强记忆能力,提高记忆效果。

3.1 视觉化记忆训练

视觉化记忆训练(visualization memorization)旨在把听到或读到的源语信息以形象化的结构、图示和画面等形式储存在大脑中,利于在回忆和表述时，能根据脑海中的画面再现语言内容。这种信息储存的方式生动形象，符合短时记忆的特点，保持时间会相应地延长，保存内容会更多、更完整。这种训练适合叙述类、描述类和介绍类的讲话。

> 技巧训练：听下列录音，进行视觉化记忆训练。要求不记笔记，先用源语进行复述，再口译成译入语。

练习一　天安门广场

（具体操作：在听的同时，大脑中要形成天安门广场的画面，包括周边建筑的名称、方位等。听完之后，通过脑海中的方位画面再现语言内容。）

练习二　中国春节

（具体操作：在听的同时，大脑中要形成人们如何准备和庆祝中国新年的画面，包括年前、年三十和大年初一人们具体的庆祝方式。听完之后，通过脑海中的情景画面再现语言内容。）

练习三　The Giant Panda

（具体操作：在听的同时，大脑中要形成大熊猫的画面，包括它的外部特征、行走姿态以及分布范围。听完之后，通过脑海中的记忆画面再现语言内容。）

练习四　Three Wishes

（具体操作：在听的同时，大脑中要形成一个故事梗概，包括农夫和他的妻子围绕三个愿望都说了什么、做了什么和结果如何。听完之后，通过脑海中的故事画面再现语言内容。）

3.2 概括性记忆训练

概括性记忆训练（outlining memorization）要求对所听内容进行逻辑分析，概括源语信息的要点及要点之间的联系，并以口译笔记为辅助，通过记住主要信息、带动细节信息的记忆方式，记住话语具体内容。这是一种对源语信息进行记忆、加工和处理的有效方法，可以减轻记忆负荷，有效提高记忆效果。

> 技巧训练：听下列录音，进行概括性记忆训练。要求记笔记，并用汉语概述原文。

练习五　孔子学院和孔子课堂

（具体操作：在听的同时，记下孔子学院和孔子课堂在英国火的几个原因。听完之后，通过要点和回忆细节信息再现语言内容。）

练习六　沉迷网络游戏的危害

（具体操作：在听的同时，记下沉迷网络游戏的几点危害和主要原因。听完之后，通过要点和回忆细节信息再现语言内容。）

练习七　The Benefits of Part-Time Jobs for College Students

（具体操作：在听的同时，记下大学生做兼职工作有几点好处。听完之后，通过要点和回忆细节信息再现语言内容。）

练习八　The Education System in the U.K.

（具体操作：在听的同时，记下英国有几个教育阶段；每个阶段的年龄划分及关键词。听完之后，通过要点和回忆细节信息再现语言内容。）

3.3 篇章结构程式化记忆训练

篇章结构程式化记忆训练（reasoning memorization）指归纳不同话语（叙述类、介绍类和论证类）的常用讲话结构，形成相对固定的篇章推理和加工模式，并结合自身的背景知识来预测讲话的主体结构，记住讲话的目的、内容和结论。具体操作时可以准备叙述类、论证类和介绍类的演讲稿，在听与理解的同时，进行有笔记练习：一是记下要点、关键词、逻辑关联词等；二是口头分析源语的层次，说出内容要点、信息点之间的逻辑关联，叙述、论证或介绍演讲的主线。

> 技巧训练：听下列录音，进行篇章结构程式化记忆训练。要求记笔记，并用汉语概述内容要点或主要思路。

练习九　寄语中国留学生

练习十　"一带一路"倡议为何受到国际社会普遍欢迎？

背景知识

"一带一路"是"丝绸之路经济带"和"二十一世纪海上丝绸之路"的简称。2013年9月和10月，中国国家主席习近平出访中亚和东南亚时，分别提出了与相关国家共同建设"丝绸之路经济带"和"二十一世纪海上丝绸之路"的倡议。该倡议以实现"政策沟通、设施联通、贸易畅通、资金融通、民心相通"为主要内容，以"共商、共建、共享"为原则，实实在在地造福沿线国家和人民。"一带一路"主要涵盖东亚、东南亚、南亚、西亚、中亚和中东欧等国家和地区。"一带一路"倡议符合有关各方共同利益，顺应地区和全球合作潮流，得到了沿线国家的积极响应。截至2020年5月，中国政府已与138个国家和30

个国际组织签署了200份共建"一带一路"合作协议。上海合作组织、东盟、亚太经合组织、欧盟、欧亚经济联盟、拉美加勒比共同体等区域合作组织,以及联合国、世界卫生组织等都表达了对"一带一路"倡议的高度支持。

练习十一　Should a Person Own a Car?

练习十二　Chinese New Year Greetings from the British Ambassador to China

第四章 口译与公共演讲

口译是一种面对面的交流，译员需要将讲话人的说话效果体现出来。这不仅要求语言内容要表述正确，也要求译员要合理地利用声音、姿势、动作和眼神等。这种可见性给译员带来许多挑战。出色的译员能通过良好的公共演讲提高听众对其翻译能力和口译质量的信任度。所以，公共演讲能力是一名优秀的译员必须具备的基本能力。译员的公共演讲能力体现在两个方面：口头表达和肢体语言。

4.1 口头表达

人在说话时，声音是最重要的工具，它会对口译的表达效果产生直接影响。正确地使用声音，可以增加讲话的分量和说服力，提高讲话的成功率。在口译过程中，译员要注意以下六个口头表达（vocal rendering）要素的运用，即发音、吐字、音量、音调、语速和停顿。

4.1.1 发音

译员的基本素质之一是发音（pronunciation）准确，语音、语调和节奏符合语言的使用规范和标准，不受地方口音的影响。

4.1.2 吐字

吐字（articulation）清楚，对于有效传递口译信息至关重要。放慢讲话速度，是加强吐字清晰度的有效方法。同时，由于正式场合的发言不同于对话交谈，它通常要求讲话人的字词发音更加完整，尽量避免字与字（词与词）之间的连读、弱读、吞音等。

4.1.3 音量

译员讲话声音的大小和强弱程度会直接影响口译的效果。适中的音量（vocal volume）使译员的口头表达更容易被听众接受，不会显得信心不足或喧宾夺主。在口译过程中，译员切忌大声喊叫，但声音也不能过小，以让在场的每个人都听清楚为宜。有时，译员需要根据发言人声音的大小、现场听众的反应来调节音量。

4.1.4 音调

在口译过程中，译员要控制好声音的高低。一般来说，译员在口译中最好采用中音，因为中音显得沉稳可信，并应注意通过音调（pitch）的变化让听众感受到友好、温和、诚恳和热情。单调不变的音调会使听众感到沉闷，从而影响口译效果。

4.1.5 语速

口头表达与一个人的语速（rate），即声音传递的快慢紧密相连。通常，中文表达速度是每分钟 150~180 字，英文则是每分钟 120~150 词。虽然译员应该考虑翻译内容的特点和讲话人采用的速度来确定自己翻译传达的节奏，但若在平均值上下浮动过大，会造成听众接收信息的额外负担。因此，译员应采用中等速度，而且在重要信息点，如数字、专门用语、人名、头衔等，以及讲话人特别强调的关键词上将速度适当放慢。在口译过程中，译员需要经常调整节奏，这是十分重要的。

4.1.6 停顿

停顿（pause）是讲话人口头表达时的标点符号，正确的停顿使听众有机会理解句子和段落的结构，同时还有时间"消化"关键短语和理解段落。对于译员来说，适当的停顿既能为自己自然大方地创造时间进行思考或修补翻译中的缺陷，又能为信息表达带来更出色的效果。但停顿时要避免加入带有个人习惯的不必要表达，如"嗯……""呃……""这个……""就是说……""你知道……""我的意思是……""对吗？""就像……""Well…""Eh…""Yes…""OK…"，等等。这些口头语会分散听众的注意力，使人感到厌烦，并给人一种缺乏准备的印象。

另外，由于译员工作时大多需要使用麦克风，嘴巴与麦克风之间最好保持一定的距离，防止音效失真和出现气爆杂音（pop noise）。同时，译员须注意不能对着麦克风喘粗气、吸鼻子、咳嗽或哗哗地翻资料等。

4.2 肢体语言

除了言语表达外，译员的身体语言（body language）同样十分重要。在口译过程中，译员应考虑以下五个方面：仪表、身体姿态、手势、眼神交流和面部表情。

4.2.1 仪表

译员要有整洁端庄、大方得体的仪容仪表（attire and appearance），这是译员精神面貌的外在体现。译员要考虑时间、地点和目的三大要素，根据工作场合选择得体的着装。在正式的谈判、会议、宴会等场合，译员需要穿着正装；在一些氛围较为轻松的场合，如游玩、参观等，译员可以穿着休闲一些的服装（business causual）。如果不能确定如何着装，译员一定要提前询问组织方。

4.2.2 身体姿态

译员要时刻保持自己的身体姿态（body posture）端正得体，自己的精神状态高度投入。例如，站立的时候切忌东倒西歪，或交叉站立、单腿独立，或懒散地倚靠在墙上、桌子旁，不要下意识地做小动作。在正式场合，切忌双手插在裤袋里，或双手交叉抱在胸前，或双手叉腰。行走时步幅不能过大，要挺胸抬头。坐姿要端庄、大方、自然，不可前倾后仰或歪歪扭扭，不能跷"二郎腿"。谈吐之间，腿脚切忌不停地抖动；同时还要注意手位和脚位，如双手应放在身体两侧，或右手搭在左手上方置于身体前侧，以及双脚应平行站立，不超过肩宽，或双脚呈 V 字形、丁字形站立等。

4.2.3 手势

作为译员，一定要端庄持重，切忌手舞足蹈。过多地使用手势（gesture）表明译员处于紧张状态，这不仅会分散听众的注意力，还会给人眼花缭乱的感觉。手势动作要适中：过大，会显得"张牙舞爪"；过小，又显得"缩手缩脚"。译员应避免习惯性和下意识动作，如抓耳挠腮、不自觉地挥舞手臂等。

4.2.4 眼神交流

在口译过程中，译员应注意与讲话人、听众的眼神交流（eye contact），这样可以加强沟通的效果。译员不能只顾埋头看笔记，而是看听众与看笔记交替进行，通过眼神交流观察听众的反应，接受他们的信息反馈。进行眼神交流时，译员要自然和从容，表现出信心和活力。如果是正式场合的演讲，译员则应和不同方位的听众进行眼神交流，而且眼神不能飘忽不定，否则给人缺乏自信的印象。

4.2.5 面部表情

译员的面部表情（facial expression）要自然真实、庄重大方、从容自信、热情友好。译员一般应面带微笑，以示友好，既要表现出对听众的善意，也应展现出自己对所译话题的兴趣和把握。译员要避免做出傲慢、沮丧、苦恼、不耐烦和无可奈何的表情，如皱眉、做鬼脸、吐舌头、叹气、一脸苦相等，也不能面无表情、冷若冰霜，使人感到压抑。

此外，在对话口译中，译员有必要了解对方的体距界域习惯，恰当地运用有利于人际交往的界域距离，如适用于公开社交场合的中庸距离80~120厘米，从而使交往者与译员处于一种和谐的心理氛围之中。

> 小组练习：四人一组，每人选择一个话题依次即兴演讲两分钟，其他人为听众，并对演讲者的口头表达和肢体语言进行评议。

- 话题一：我理想中的大学。
- 话题二：我理想中的老师。
- 话题三：大学生如何平衡学习和娱乐？
- 话题四：大学生的职责是什么？
- 话题五：如何避免校园欺凌？

> 课堂练习：两人一组，每人准备一个三分钟中文或英文演讲进行模拟口译。其中一人进行演讲，另一人进行连续口译。班级其他成员为听众，并对每组人员的口头表达和肢体语言进行评议。

（话题可以是有关新闻事件、某个公众人物等的介绍。演讲过程中，各小组成员允许使用大纲或笔记，但不能逐词逐句地读稿。完成一轮模拟口译后，各小组成员重新组合、变换角色，直至所有成员均完成演讲和口译任务。）

课后作业：用手机拍摄自己在"课堂练习"中的演讲视频，审视自己的口头表达、肢体语言是否存在问题，并思考相应的改进方法。

第五章 口译的译前准备与预测

口译的第一步是听取信息，对源语进行听辨、分析和理解。这个信息接收过程不是被动的，译员在全神贯注地听的同时，可以结合自己对口译语境和讲话人背景的了解，进行合理的分析和预测。只有这样，译员才能更好地跟上讲话人的思路，缓解"听"的压力，使口译过程更轻松、口译理解更准确。

5.1 口译的译前准备

译员在口译前进行相应的准备是为了更好地理解、分析和预测讲话内容。为了做好口译工作，译员必须进行三个方面的充分准备，即长期准备、近期准备和临场准备。

5.1.1 长期准备

从根本上提高自己的口译水平，译员需要长期积累各方面的知识。首先，译员必须具有良好的语言功底，其中包括对语音、语调、字词、句子、语义以及篇章的掌握，只有这样，口译时才能传神达意。其次，译员应该培养良好的学习习惯，保持对事物的广泛兴趣，尽量涉猎不同的专业，扩大自己的知识面和增强自己的理解能力，不断积累并更新自己的词汇和表达方式，进行多方面知识的长期积累。最后，译员还要熟练地掌握口译技巧，包括当众演讲、口译预测、话语分析与理解、短期记忆、记笔记、译数字、复述、习语翻译、意义重组与表达、应变策略等。

5.1.2 近期准备

在接到某个主题的口译任务之后，了解该主题的论题、背景、内容和术语等，并为此做好精心准备是十分有必要的。这主要包括三个方面。一是词汇准备。译员需要提前熟悉和掌握术语、固定词组与生词，比如搜集专业词汇与专有名词，制作一个专业词汇与专有名词中英文对照表，包括姓名、头衔、单位等，并重点标注不熟悉的字词、术语。二是套语和套话准备。译员有必要熟记一些套话、习惯用语，这样可以节省时间和精力，如一些固有表达：迎来送往的寒暄，礼仪祝词的开场白、结束语，等等。三是背景知识准备。背景知识包括所涉领域的基本概念和专业知识、讲话人的教育背景和工作背景等。译员可以通过查询相关网站等方式寻找有用信息，以自行准备背景材料和提前标注一些重要内容。一般在会议开始之前，主办方会给译员一些资料，其中包括会议议程，与会人员的名单、头衔、履历和联系方式，相关公司的背景材料，谈判时各方的提问，部分发言稿或内容摘要，等等。译员可以通过阅读这些资料和联系与会人员来获得想要的信息。

5.1.3 临场准备

在做某场具体的口译之前，译员一定要带好相关的资料、文具、设备等。译员最好提前30分钟到达工作地点，熟悉工作环境，如房间设施情况、有无麦克风等。为了获得良好的沟通效果，译员可以充分利用会谈或会议开始前后的时间、茶歇时间以及用餐时间，主动与主办方和发言人沟通，及时更新信息。在会谈或会议进行中，译员需要敏锐地捕捉信息，及时地调整自己的用词和译文，以符合双方的用语习惯。

5.2 口译的预测

预测（anticipation）是译员在口译过程中为增强理解而普遍采用的策略。它通过激活储存在长期记忆中的背景知识，促进译员在听的过程中对意义的理解。Lederer 把预测归为下列三种情况：

- 预测惯用语句、语言的固定搭配（the early recognition of a formula）；
- 预测讲话人的说话思路（a logical sequence of ideas, which makes the perception of words almost unnecessary）；
- 预测整个语篇的论点及逻辑思维论证（discursive arguments or logical sequences, which have been heard before albeit expressed in different terms）。

（Lederer, 1981, 引自 Setton, 1999：53）

合理的预测可以节约译员对源语进行分析和整合的时间，使其能更合理地分配注意力，达到更好的理解效果。口译的预测包括语言预测和非语言预测。

5.2.1 语言预测

口译的语言预测是根据语言知识，包括词的搭配、句子结构、交际语境等来预测将要听到的内容。在任何语言中，句子结构、字词的搭配顺序都有一定的规律可循。例如，在英语和汉语句子中，主语、谓语和宾语的词序基本上是一致的，但时间或地点状语之间的排列顺序有差异：英语是从小到大，汉语则是从大到小；英语单词作定语时，除了个别后置之外，其他通常和汉语一样放在所修饰的单词之前；在字词搭配上，英语介词后面接冠词或名词的概率很高，接另一个介词或动词的概率则很低；英文 the 的后边跟名词或形容词，不可能跟动词。此外，英汉丰富的固定词组搭配有利于译员进行语言预测。例如：

- Business people in both countries profit from the open economies we are building according to the rules of the WTO.

我们两国的工商界人士均受益于我们按照世贸组织原则建设的开放型经济。

当译员听到 profit 时，可预测后边将是 from，介词宾语将是与经济有关，因为主语是两国的工商界人士；当听到 according 时，可预测后边将是 to。又如：

- Katie was green with envy when she saw that you got a new car for your birthday present.

  看到你的生日礼物是一辆新车时，凯蒂满怀嫉妒。

当听到 She is green with 时，译员马上可以预测后边将是 envy，因为 green with envy 是一个英语习语。又如：

- 中国政府将采取一切措施来解决这个问题。

  The Chinese government will take all measures to solve this problem.

当听到"采取"时，译员会预测后边将是"措施"或"办法"；当听到"解决"时，他会预测后边将是"问题"等。另外，部分寒暄语（如问候、介绍、欢迎、感谢和告别）和套语套话（如表示赞同、反对等），在特定场合中都有固定的表达方式。译员需要训练自己在遇到生字词、同音词、一词多义、习语和固定搭配时，能根据上下文语境、词素和词源来分析并找到词义，从而理解所听到的内容。

5.2.2 非语言预测

口译的非语言预测是根据非语言知识（百科知识、专业知识、情景知识等）提前预测讲话的目的、内容和结论。

在开始每次具体的口译工作之前，译员需要做相应的准备，其中包括预测讲话内容和讲话人的基本情况。讲话人的身份和背景通常决定其讲话的目的、对事物的观点和看法。在口译前，译员应该准备以下问题：讲话人是谁？是什么身份？他有什么观点？这次讲话的目的是什么？……

正确的预测会使译员跟着讲话人的思路走,更好地理解讲话内容。

预测是口译活动中非常重要的内容和技巧之一,它是一种有意识的认知思维活动,与译员的知识结构和逻辑分析能力有着紧密的联系。有效的预测是译员语言知识与非语言知识共同发生作用的结果,它在口译过程中起着非常重要的作用。译员提前预测、同步理解讲话人的讲话内容,不但有利于减轻自己的记忆负荷,同时也利于提高口译的准确性。

> 课后作业:根据下列情景预测口译内容,做译前准备。

练习一 中国国家主席习近平会见英国四十八家集团俱乐部主席斯蒂芬·佩里

练习二 中国驻英国大使馆刘晓明大使在官邸同英国约克公爵安德鲁王子共庆新春

5.3 迎来送往口译

5.3.1 迎来送往译前准备

A. 词汇

- foreign affairs office
- chief of the protocol office
- at the invitation of…
- in a(n) private/official capacity
- the usual change of greetings
- itinerary/schedule
- welcome speech / speech of welcome

- reception/entertainment party

- buffet reception

- farewell speech

- to make a customs declaration

- to go through the exit/entry/customs formalities

- to pay a(n) state/official/goodwill/working visit to…

- to meet somebody at the airport/railway station

- to see somebody off at the airport/railway station

- to be headed/led by…

- to hold/give/host a banquet in honor of…

- to extend kind/cordial hospitality to…

- to bid farewell to…

- to say goodbye to…

- to convey the cordial greetings and best wishes of…to…

- in a cordial and friendly atmosphere

- in an earnest and frank atmosphere

- to be about to conclude someone's friendly visit

- to pay a courtesy/farewell call to…

B. 套语套话

- Allow me to introduce myself. I am…

- Excuse me, but aren't you…?

- How do you do? Welcome to China.

- It's a great pleasure to have you here with us.

- I'm so pleased to have met you.

- It's been my pleasure in meeting you.

- I'm glad/happy/delighted to have the pleasure of meeting you in…

- This is our first meeting. I'm glad to meet you.

- Is it your first visit to China?

- I still remember our last meeting.

- Thank you for coming all the way to…

- I'm honored to have this opportunity to welcome all of you.

- It is a great pleasure for me to welcome you all to…

- It gives me great pleasure to welcome all of you to…

- We appreciate very much that you have come to visit our city in spite of the long and tiring journey.

- How was your journey?

- How was the flight?

- Have you had a pleasant flight?

- I am glad to have the honor of introducing…

- I'd like to introduce you to…

- May I introduce you to…?

- I'd like you to meet…

- I have long wanted to visit your country, and I am so glad to come this time.

- We'll do our best to make your stay here a pleasant one.

- As soon as we arrive in your beautiful country, we feel very much at home.

- Thank you for such thoughtful arrangement for us.

- Thank you very much for inviting me to this delightful dinner.

- Wish you all the best in your tour/visit.

- Wish your visit a complete success

- I wish you a pleasant stay here.
- How do you like today's visit?
- What do you think of the scenery here?
- We have prepared an activity for you. I hope you will like it.
- Is there anything else that is of interest to you?
- I hope you have enjoyed the visit.
- You are about to conclude your visit. How do you like the visit?
- We have enjoyed our visit here in the past few days.
- I'm impressed by the beautiful scenery here.
- We are deeply moved by your warm reception.
- Thank you for your thoughtful arrangement and warm hospitality.
- With a sense of infinite regret, we bid farewell today.
- I'm looking forward to your visit again / the opportunity of hosting you here again.
- It's very nice of you to come all the way to see me off.
- Let's keep in touch.
- You are welcome to visit China at your convenience.
- Hope to see each other again soon.
- Remember me to…
- Say hello to…for me.
- Take care.
- I wish you a pleasant journey.
- Have a nice trip!
- Have a safe trip home!

C. 练习三至练习五对话口译预测和译前准备

- 曼彻斯特火车站英方迎接中方参会人员。
- 北京大兴国际机场迎接到访外国客人。
- 英方官员在中国春节期间宴请中方客人。

5.3.2 迎来送往对话口译

迎来送往是接待活动中最重要的环节。对话内容无外乎是自我介绍，表示问候、欢迎，介绍活动日程，表示感谢、告别，以及谈话双方根据即时情景进行的交流，等等。谈话的双方为使交流顺利地进行，一定会遵循 2.4.1 节中提到的对话合作和联想法则。如果译员能跟上谈话人的思路，抓住上下文的逻辑进行联想和预测，就能快速、准确理解谈话内容，为成功完成口译任务创造有利条件。

> 小组练习：三人一组，分别担任中文、英文对话者和口译员，进行交替口译练习。练习时注意转换角色。

练习三

A: Welcome to Manchester, Mr. Ma.

B: 感谢您亲自到车站来接我。火车基本正点，希望没让您等很久。

A: How was your journey?

B: 很好。从伦敦到曼城只有 2 个小时的车程。我记得我上一次在伦敦，大约是 18 年前，从伦敦坐火车到曼城是 4 个小时。

A: Yes, on the London-Manchester Line, the train runs nearly 200 miles per hour. I think it is the fastest one in the U.K. Trains run much slower on other lines. I wonder whether you have noticed that the train actually tilts.

B: 的确。没有中国高铁那么稳。我本想在火车上读会儿报纸，但火车运行不太稳，只好作罢。

A: How long did you serve in the U.K. in your last post? Have you noticed any changes of the U.K. in this post?

B: 我上一个任期是 3 年。英国有变化，但变化不大。也可能是英国城市规划要求，一般不轻易改变临街风貌，经常是"修旧如旧"。

A: Agreed. Well, thank you for accepting our invitation at short notice.

B: 谢谢您的邀请，这是我的荣幸。

A: It's a 10-minute walk from the station to your hotel. If you don't mind, we will walk to the restaurant I booked. It is half way to the hotel.

B: 太好了，感谢您的精心安排。

练习四

A: 欢迎到北京考察，一路上都好吧？

B: Yes, a wonderful trip. I watched a new movie on the way and had a good nap afterwards. Thank you for meeting me at the airport.

A: 这是我的荣幸。这是您第一次来北京吗？

B: No, I am fortunate to have visited Beijing many times. But no matter how often I visit, I never cease to be amazed with the level of change that is taking place here. This new airport, for instance, is very impressive.

A: 是啊，北京大兴国际机场于 2019 年正式投入运营，人们称它为北京新机场，是北京市的第二座国际机场。

B: It's very modern and huge. I heard it is the world's largest airport terminal. What is the capacity of the airport?

A: 预计到 2021 年，每年可以接待旅客 4 500 万人次，未来将达到 1 亿人次。

B: Great! This will greatly reduce the pressure on other airports in Beijing.

A: 您说得对。该机场位于北京和河北省廊坊市交界处，有望满足北京、天津和河北地区的需求。

B: What about the ground transportation?

A: 这里有高铁、城铁、地铁和机场专线巴士，将新机场与北京和其他主要地区快速、高效地联通在一起。到北京市中心，坐城铁只需 20 分钟，坐大兴机场地铁线只需 19 分钟。当然，也可以打车或租车。

B: It is very convenient.

A: 是的，北京的变化非常大。希望您有时间可以游览北京，也祝您访问愉快。

B: Sure.

练习五

 背景知识

特拉法加广场（Trafalgar Square）是位于伦敦市中心的著名广场，地理位置十分优越。广场南面是著名的白厅大街，如果要去议会大厦，这里是必经之地。广场北面是国家美术馆，东北角是著名的圣马丁教堂。西南面是海军部拱门，穿过拱门则是通往白金汉宫的林荫大道。周边还有加拿大、南非等英联邦国家的高级专员署（英联邦国家互派的大使级代表处）。这座广场是为纪念历史上著名的特拉法加港海战而修建的，广场中部是两个花形喷水池，南侧耸立着英国传奇海军名将纳尔逊的纪念碑，碑身青铜浮雕反映了 1805 年英国海军战胜法国海军的场面，碑座四周是四只巨型铜狮。两百多年来，特拉法加广场一直是伦敦乃至全英人民聚会、举办庆祝活动的场地。

特拉法加广场春节庆典，由伦敦华埠商会主办，2003 年首次举办，是亚洲地区以外规模最大的春节庆典活动。如今，该庆典已成为伦敦每年的特色活动之一，深受在英华侨华人和当地民众的喜爱。成千上万的人会在庆典当日涌入这里，观看中国春节传统庆祝活动，品尝中国传统小吃。当天有花车巡游、舞龙舞狮表演等活动，伦敦本地华裔和来自中国的艺术家们还会在特拉法加广场的春节主舞台上表演舞蹈、音乐等精彩节目。

A: Good evening. Very nice to have you here with us. Hope you will have a good time here.

B: 谢谢，非常高兴到贵府作客。

A: I heard you just celebrated your Spring Festival. Happy New Year to you and all the best in a prosperous year.

B: 谢谢！连日来，英国各地纷纷举办春节庆祝活动，到处都充满了节日的欢乐气氛。

A: You are right. Prime Minister May hosted the Chinese New Year celebration reception a few days ago. No.10 Downing Street was decorated with traditional couplets and lanterns. The Prime Minister did a paper cutting of the Chinese character "spring" and joined members of the Chinese community in the "Lion Eye Dotting Ceremony".

B: 昨天，我们还在特拉法加广场成功举办了亚洲地区以外的规模最大的春节庆典活动，有70万英国民众和游客参加了此次活动。春节已成为中英两国人民的共同节日。

A: I totally agree with you. At present, China-U.K. relationship is developing steadily, and the cooperation in various fields between the two countries continues to advance.

B: 是的，今年是中华人民共和国成立70周年，也是中英建立代办级外交关系65周年，希望中英各界携手努力，将中英关系的大厦建得更加坚固！

A: I hope so, too. The City of London will host a special celebration for the 70th anniversary of the founding of the People's Republic of China and will invite people from business and trade sectors of the two countries to participate.

B: 谢谢！近年来，伦敦金融城积极开展对华合作，取得丰硕成果。希望金融城抓住"一带一路"机遇，进一步深化对华合作，为中英"黄金时代"做出新的更大的贡献。

A: The Belt and Road Initiative has brought important opportunities to the U.K.

I will lead a delegation to China in March to promote cooperation in the fields of fintech, green finance, and innovation.

B: 预祝您访华成功！

> 小组练习：三人一组，自行设计口译情景，并分别扮演不同的角色，进行对话口译练习。练习时注意转换角色。

示例角色：

张院长：某大学经管学院院长

Emily Sewell：英国某大学招生办负责人

李莉：口译员

（双方寒暄，比如天气、城市、学校情况等。根据之前的电子邮件沟通，双方商讨签订MOU、互派留学生交流学习等事宜。）

第六章　口译笔记

口译笔记是指在口译过程中，译员用简单的字、词、缩写或符号快速记下的关键信息。其目的在于提醒相关的口译内容和讲话逻辑，增强译员的短期记忆，减轻其工作时的记忆负荷。

6.1 口译笔记特点

口译笔记的即时性特点决定其不同于秘书做会议记录或学生听课记笔记。由于口译的限时性，口译笔记不能用速记法，因为速记法采用的是一套完全不同的符号系统，自身还需要解码，而译员很难分出时间与注意力来解码速记符号。口译笔记也不像学生的听课笔记，为课后复习、阅读、考试之用。口译笔记只供译员在口译现场使用，一般不会在口译工作结束之后再度使用，也不会供他人阅读。因此，在口译过程中，译员只需要记住那些对自己起到提示作用的信息即可，没有必要、也做不到记下讲话的所有内容。事实上，如果译员花费过多时间在记笔记上，他将无法有足够的时间对听取的内容进行理解和分析，以及思考如何进行语言的转换，也可能错过后面的信息，或是没有足够的时间考虑如何用译入语进行正确的表达。

6.2 口译笔记内容

正确记笔记可以忠实地传递口译信息。译员在记笔记时，首要任务是对源语进行逻辑分析，抓住主要观点，记下关键词。其次是记下表示内容前因后果、上下文逻辑关系的关联词，如"但是""因此""只要"等。再次要记下讲话人共讲了几个观点，以免遗漏信息。同时，译员要注意动词的时态、语态，记笔记时要连同动词的时态，包括虚拟、条件、假设等，特别是情态动词一并记录，因为情态动词对其他动词的功能起决定性作用。最后，对于那些不能记住或根本不想花精力去记的内容，译员可以依靠记笔记来减轻记忆负荷，如数字、地点、日期、组织机构名称、清单、目录等。只要能够提示讲话内容，笔记应该是越少越好。

6.3 如何记口译笔记

一个合格的译员必须能够科学地记笔记，所记内容应清楚、易读，并且一目了然。口译笔记一般竖着记，把一句话分成几个意群，如主语、谓语、宾语等。一个字、一个缩写或一个符号就占据一行，从上到下倾斜成阶梯结构。这种结构形象地体现出上下文的逻辑结构，简化译员的思维过程。当一句话或一个话题结束后，译员可以画一条斜线或两个分隔线"//"，以免前后内容混淆。

关于是用源语还是用译入语记笔记，学术界没有绝对的规则，这取决于译员的个人习惯。两者各有利弊。当使用源语记笔记时，特别是遇到源语特有的文化或概念内容时，译员可以直接记下，不必考虑翻译的问题；不利的一面是译员有时会被动地听什么、记什么，忽略对源语话语进行真正的理解和分析，当进行口译时却发现没有真正地理解源语内容，从而无法进行译入语的再表达。当译员用译入语记笔记时，他不得不对所听内容进行加工、整理，真正理解脱离源语语言外壳的意义，使笔记成为译文的雏形，为表达提供便利。这就是为什么很多译员偏好用译入语记

第六章　口译笔记

笔记。实际上，出于方便，译员可以兼用两种语言，甚至使用任何方式记笔记。唯一的标准是快速、清晰和准确。

6.3.1 口译笔记的符号

在口译笔记中使用符号是为了节省记笔记的时间，能在最短时间内唤起记忆，将其复原成完整的信息，从而提高记笔记的效率。将文字内容简化为符号可以避免字对字的翻译。口译笔记符号应该简单明了、符合逻辑，并形成体系。译员建立一套属于自己的个性化符号系统是非常有必要的。以下介绍一些常用的笔记符号。

表 6–1　常用笔记符号：箭头类

符号	汉语释义	英语释义
→	出口、到达、导致、交给、造成、发给、派遣……	export to, arrive in, lead to, present to, give to, result in, send to, cause…
←	来自、源于、进口、收到……	come from, import from, receive from…
↑	发展、上升、增长、扩大、提高、增强、起飞、发射、升级、升值……	develop, rise, go up, strengthen, increase, ascend, skyrocket…
↓	下降、降低、减少、下调、削减、贬值……	drop, decrease, descend, go down, reduce…
↗	越来越好、渐渐好转、逐渐上升、持续上扬……	getting better, going upward, moving up, becoming better and better…
↘	逐渐下降、不断下跌、不断亏损、逐渐减少……	dropping, falling, declining…

表 6–2　常用笔记符号：数学、物理符号类

符号	汉语释义	英语释义
+	增加、此外、额外、加上……	additional, new, increase…
=	等同、相同、即、对手……	equal to, the same as, correspond to, is, are, mean, that is to say, in other words, a match, a rival, a competitor, a counterpart…
−	减去、少……	without, minus, decrease, lack, in short of, in shortage of…
≈	大约、约等于……	about, around, or so, approximately…
<	少于、小于、低于……	less than, smaller, inferior to…
>	多于、大于、高于、优于、超过……	more than, bigger, larger, greater, better than, superior to, surpass…
≠	不同、无敌……	be different from, matchless, peerless…
∵	因为	because, due to, thanks to, because of…
∴	所以	therefore, so…
×	错的、不对的、不好的、失误、坏……	wrong, incorrect, something bad, notorious, negative…

表 6–3　常用笔记符号：标点符号类

符号	汉语释义	英语释义
:	说、解释、宣布……	speak, say, talk, explain, announce, declare…

第六章 口译笔记

（续表）

符号	汉语释义	英语释义
.	表示时间。这个"."的位置不同，表示的时间概念不一样。例如，"d"表示"今天"，".d"表示"昨天"，"d."表示"明天"。以此类推，"y"表示"今年"，"..y"表示"前年"；"m"表示"月"，".2m"表示"2个月前"……	
?	问题、疑问……	question, issue…
( )	在……之间、包括、在……之内……	among, within…

表 6-4　其他常用笔记符号

符号	汉语释义	英语释义
√	正确、好、对的、确定的、著名的……	correct, right, good, affirmative, certain, sure, well-known, famous…
○	人	person, people…
∧	引领、领导……	lead, manage…
⊙	会议、讨论、谈判……	meeting, meet, conference, discussion, negotiation…
☆	最好的、杰出的、最佳的、重要的、模范……	best, outstanding, excellent, important, model…
□	国家	country, state, nation…
∪	合同	agreement, accord, treaty, contract…
⊥	分歧	dispute…
△	代表	on behalf of, represent…
#	讲话结束、数字……	finish one's talk, number …

（续表）

符号	汉语释义	英语释义
&	和、与、陪同、另外……	and, together with, along with, accompany, along with, further, more…
∈	属于	belong to…

一旦采用某个符号并赋予其特定含义，译员就可以根据这个符号构建其他符号。例如，如果符号 x 表示"时间"，则可以使用以下变体：

表 6–5　笔记符号 x 的变体

符号	汉语释义	英语释义	符号	汉语释义	英语释义
$x-$	永久的	timeless, eternal	xx	多次、经常	many times, often
$2x$	两倍	twice	$+x$	更多（长）时间	more time, longer time
$=x$	同等时间	equal time	xtx	偶尔	from time to time, occasionally
$100x$	100 倍	a hundred times	$ltdx$	时间有限	a limited time
$oldx$	以前的、旧式的	old-time, old fashioned	gdx	美好时光	have a good time
$x>$	将来	future	$<x$	过去	past

6.3.2　口译笔记的缩写

缩略语是短语或词的全称的缩写形式。由于其省时、省力，缩略语在口译笔记中被广泛使用。

1. 英文缩写

英文缩写可以遵循下列原则：

A. 去掉所有元音，只留辅音。例如：

- hotel → htl
- because → bcs
- believe → blv
- building → bldg

B. 只保留前几个字母。例如：

- attention → att
- acknowledge → ack
- alternate → alt
- application → app

C. 只保留首字母和最后一个字母。例如：

- your → yr
- from → fm
- room → rm
- doctor → Dr

D. 音节缩写。例如：

- answer → ans
- company → co
- facsimile → fax
- examination → exam
- government → gov
- influenza → flu
- laboratory → lab

- mathematics → math
- memorandum → memo
- punishment → pun
- service → serv
- telephone → phone
- purchase → pur
- international → int
- police → pol

E. 根据发音缩写单词。例如：

- you → u
- are → r
- through → thru
- though → tho
- see → c

F. 简化词的后缀。例如：

- able/-ible/-ble → bl
- available → avlbl
- possible → psbl
- cable → cbl
- double → dbl

G. 用首字母简化词组。例如：

- as soon as possible → asap
- as a matter of fact → amof
- as follow → af
- as quick as possible → aqap

第六章 口译笔记

- for your reference → fyr
- all the best → atb
- as early as possible → aeap
- at the moment → atm
- as far as I concerned → afaic
- gross national product → gnp
- as far as I know → afaik
- gross domestic product → gdp
- as far as I understand it → afaiui
- in case of → ico
- as I said before → aisb
- official use only → ouo
- as I see it → aisi
- also known as → aka
- take your time → tyt
- as much as possible → amap
- normal trade relations → ntr
- all my best wishes → ambw
- do it yourself → diy
- estimated time of arrival → eta
- be right back → brb
- if I recall/remember correctly → iirc
- laugh out loud → lol
- no problem → np
- thank you → ty
- with regard to → wrt

- in my opinion → imo
- in other words → iow
- for example → e.g.
- for instance → i.e.

H. 用数字代替英文发音。例如：

- one-to-one → 121
- too good to be true → 2gtbt
- too easy → 2ez
- tomorrow → 2moro

2. 汉语缩写

汉语缩写可以遵循下列原则：

A. 语素缩写，即由词语、短语中的词或语素构成缩略语。例如：

- 北京大学 → 北大
- 改革开放 → 改开
- 扫除文盲 → 扫盲
- 人民警察 → 民警
- 欧洲联盟 → 欧盟
- 中国共产党 → 中共
- 奥林匹克运动 → 奥运
- 中央电视台 → 中央台

B. 中心词缩写，即由原词语的核心词构成缩略语。例如：

- 人造地球卫星 → 人造卫星
- 中国共产党第十九次全国代表大会 → 中共十九大
- 中国人民政治协商会议 → 政协

- 中华人民共和国国家发展和改革委员会 → 发改委
- 中国科学院 → 中科院
- 全国人大常委会 → 人大
- 亚洲基础设施投资银行 → 亚投行

C. 合并缩写，即归纳原词语中的并列词与数量词构成缩略语。例如：

- 世界观、人生观、价值观 → 三观
- 农业、工业、国防和科学技术的现代化 → 四个现代化 / 四化
- 中国特色社会主义道路自信、理论自信、制度自信、文化自信 → 四个自信
- 全面建成小康社会、全面深化改革、全面依法治国、全面从严治党 → 四个全面
- 政策沟通、设施联通、贸易畅通、资金融通、民心相通 → 五通

每位译员的记忆、思维和逻辑方式都是独一无二的，在记笔记方面的天赋也各不相同。一些译员可能记忆力特别好，一些译员可能对某个领域或主题特别熟悉，一些译员可能擅长做笔记。毋庸置疑，每位译员记笔记的内容和符号也会各异。因此，对于初学者来说，不建议机械地照搬其他译员记笔记的方法。只有通过反复练习，并在实践中不断完善，才能发展出一套符合自己特点和习惯的且行之有效的记笔记方法。

6.3.3 口译笔记样例

样例一

原文

I was deeply impressed during my trip to Tianjin in September this year for the Summer Davos and benefited a lot from the conference. China's integrated development of Beijing, Tianjin, and Hebei offers great reference to the U.K.

笔记

  impress
    → Tianjin/ 9 月
     Davos ☉
     Benefit./
  BJ-TJ-HB
    ↓
   UK//

译文

  今年 9 月赴华出席的天津夏季达沃斯世界经济论坛给我留下了深刻印象，令人受益匪浅。中国政府推动京津冀一体化发展的经验值得英方借鉴。

样例二

原文

  首先，我要表达我深切和诚挚的谢意，感谢邀请我今天上午在这里发言。对一个中国学者来说，能够与你们一起庆祝这个重要的庆典是我巨大的荣幸。

笔记

  TKS
    → invit.
      :/
  中学者
    honor ↓
    庆典 //

译文

I first want to express my profound and sincere thanks for the invitation to speak here this morning. It is an enormous privilege for a Chinese scholar to join with you in celebrating this grand ceremony.

样例三

原文

To tour in China is many foreigners' dream, because China is an ancient civilized country with a long history and rich culture. We all should know more about it. We can visit the world-famous scenic spots and historical sites, and enjoy the Chinese operas and acrobatic shows as well as the Chinese cuisine and local delicacies. Most importantly, we have a sense of how ordinary people lead their life.

笔记

    →中 tral.

      Dream/

    ↓

    古

    历史＋文

      了解/

    ↓

    名胜

    戏剧

    杂技

    小吃

      feel→生活//

译文

来中国旅游是许多外国人的梦想,因为中国是一个文明古国,有着悠久的历史和灿烂的文化,值得我们进行更多深入的了解。我们可以游览中国的名胜古迹,欣赏中国的戏剧和杂技表演,品尝中国美食和地方小吃,同时还有机会感受人们的生活状况。

样例四

原文

值此首届世界互联网大会开幕之际,我谨代表中国政府和中国人民,并以我个人的名义,向会议的召开致以热烈的祝贺!向出席会议的各国政府官员、国际机构负责人专家学者以及企业家等各方嘉宾,表示热烈的欢迎!

笔记

$$1^{st}\ Internet\ \odot$$
$$\triangle\ 中\ G+\ °\ +I$$
$$\rightarrow\ \odot\ open$$
$$祝贺/$$
$$\rightarrow\ 各\ G\ °$$
$$负责\ °\rightarrow int.+org.$$
$$guests \rightarrow exp.+学\ °+busi\ °$$
$$welcome//$$

译文

On the occasion of the opening of the First World Internet Conference, on behalf of the Chinese government and Chinese people and in my own name, I would like to extend warm congratulations on the Conference. I also want to extend a warm welcome to all participants, including government officials from various countries, heads of international institutions, experts, scholars, and business people.

第六章　口译笔记

> 技巧训练：听下列录音，进行有笔记口译训练。

练习一　英译汉（1—5）

练习二　汉译英（1—5）

6.4 礼仪祝词口译

6.4.1 礼仪祝词译前准备

A. 表示称谓

- 尊敬的：honorable, distinguished, respected…
- 主席 / 董事长：president, chairman, chairperson…
- 亲爱的朋友们：dear friends
- 女士们、先生们：ladies and gentlemen
- 陛下：Your Majesty
- 殿下：Your Royal Highness
- 阁下：Your Honor/Excellency

B. 表示职位头衔

- 总：chief, general, head, prime…
- 副：vice, associate, assistant, deputy…
- 助理：assistant
- 常务：managing, executive
- 执行：executive

- 名誉：honorary
- 代理：acting
- 董事长/董事会主席：Chairman of the Board
- 副校长（在英国实为校长，相当于美国大学的 President）：Vice Chancellor

C. 表示欢迎

- On behalf of…, I am delighted to welcome all of you…
- It is my pleasant duty to extend to you a cordial welcome on behalf of…
- It is a real honor and privilege for us to welcome you to…
- It is with a profound feeling of pleasure and privilege that, on behalf of…, I extend a hearty welcome to you all, especially to the distinguished guests from…
- As the chairperson of this symposium, I have the pleasure and honor of welcoming all of you to this international meeting.
- May I welcome all of you to…
- On behalf of…, I bid a warm welcome to you all gathering here to participate…
- May I begin by welcoming you to…

D. 表示感谢

- I'd like to thank…
- I wish to thank…
- We deeply appreciate your coming to…
- My special thanks must go to…(who…)
- I'd like to express my deepest gratitude to…
- I would like to offer my heartfelt thanks to…
- My sincere thanks must go to…

- We are particularly grateful to…
- I'd like to pay tribute to…

E. 表示祝酒

- Propose a toast.
- Drink to…
- To…
- To raise our glasses to…
- I would like to invite you to join me in a toast…

6.4.2 礼仪祝词连续口译

礼仪祝词（ceremonial speeches）的结构特征大致由五部分组成：第一是称谓，根据与会人的身份而定；第二是表达愉快、荣幸、欢迎、问候、感谢、祝贺等；第三是通过某种修辞手法（引用、幽默、轶事、现实情景联想等）吸引听众的注意力，增进情感和友谊，引出正式话题；第四是主体部分，谈话与主题相关，如以往的成绩及其作用、意义，目前的发展情况，将来的目标、任务、使命等，并阐述观点，表明立场和态度等；第五是表达祝愿、祝酒等，并结束讲话。

课堂练习：听下列录音，进行有笔记连续口译训练。

练习三 **A Speech by Her Majesty the Queen at the China State Banquet, 2015**

 背景知识

Buckingham Palace today is the London residence and administrative headquarter of the Monarch. It is recognized around the world as the place where national and royal celebrations are held, and where people can watch the regular Changing the Guard ceremony. Her Majesty also holds weekly audiences with the Prime Minister and receives newly-appointed foreign ambassadors at Buckingham Palace. The State Rooms at Buckingham Palace are open to visitors for 10 weeks every summer.

练习四　习近平主席在上海合作组织青岛峰会欢迎宴会上的祝酒辞

 背景知识

上海合作组织（Shanghai Cooperation Organization），简称"上合组织"（SCO），成立于2001年6月15日，是由中国、俄罗斯、哈萨克斯坦、吉尔吉斯斯坦、塔吉克斯坦、乌兹别克斯坦、印度和巴基斯坦8个国家组成的一个永久性政府间国际组织。2018年6月9日至10日，上海合作组织青岛峰会在山东省青岛市举办；会上签署了《上海合作组织成员国元首理事会青岛宣言》。

第七章 句子口译技巧

英语和汉语属于两种不同的语系，受不同文化的影响，在语言表达方面各自有鲜明的特点。英语句子可划分为简单句、并列句和复合句，句子结构通常呈"葡萄藤"式，通过主句加从句、非谓语动词和名词短语等作为附属成分来表达。汉语则呈线形排列，短句较多，句子结构呈"竹子"型。英汉互译时须充分考虑两种语言各自的结构特点，保证译入语符合逻辑，言语通顺、流畅、自然、地道。

7.1 句子拆分与合并技巧

英语强调形合，逻辑清晰，结构比较严密，因此长句较多。汉语强调意合，语义和逻辑关系常隐含在字里行间，结构比较松散，因此简单句较多。所以通常情况下，在英译汉时，为了顺应汉语的语言结构特点和句法修辞原则，需要把一个长而复杂的英语句子拆译成若干个较短、较简单的汉语句子。在汉译英时，则需要分析汉语句子的意义，确定句子的结构和形式，把若干个汉语的短句合译成英语的长句，这样才能顺应英语语言表达的需要。

7.1.1 主句、从句拆分与合并

英语的复合句由主句加上从句构成，从句包括主语从句、宾语从句、表语从句、同位语从句、定语从句（限定性和非限定性定语从句）以及状语从句（时间、地点、原因、结果、条件、目的和让步状语从句）。在英译汉时，需要分析英语句子的结构和形式，在必要的情况下，在英语原句的意群切断处，把主句和从句拆译成汉语的简单句；反之，在汉译英时，可以把汉语的多个简单句合并成英语主句加从句的形式。例如：

英译汉

- I wish to thank you for the incomparable hospitality **for which** the Chinese people are justly famous throughout the world.

  我要感谢你们无与伦比的盛情款待，中国人民正是以这种热情好客而闻名世界。（定语从句拆分）

- It was an attack that shocked Britain and made us question the morality of our society **where** such a terrible thing could happen to such a good person.

  这个事件震惊了英国，不得不让我们质疑整个社会的道德体系。如此可怕的事情怎么会发生在这么一个好人身上。（定语从句拆分）

- City Plan 2019-2040 is one of a number of changes the council is making **so that** the planning process is more transparent and easier to understand.

  2019—2040城市规划是市政府正在进行的一系列变革之一。只有这样，整个规划过程才会更加透明，更易于理解。（主从复合句拆分）

- From a young age she was fascinated with hills and mountains, partly thanks to the high school she attended in a town on the edge of the Peak District, **which** encouraged pupils to take up outdoor pursuits.

  她从小就对爬山着迷，部分原因是她在峰区边缘的一个小镇上念的高中。这个学校鼓励学生从事户外活动。（非限定性定语从句拆分）

- It is said that there are three types of people—**those who** wait for things to happen, **those who** make things happen, and **those who** ask what happened.

  据说世界上有三种不同类型的人：第一类人总是在等待事情发生，第二类人会促成事情发生，第三类人询问发生了什么事。（表语从句拆分）

汉译英

- 中华文明历经 5 000 多年没有中断，延绵至今。这在世界古代文明中是唯一的。

  The Chinese civilization has continued uninterruptedly for over 5,000 years, **which** is unique among the world's ancient civilizations.（定语从句合并）

- 这是一次很好的生活经历：失败是成功之母。

  It is a good life lesson **that** defeat can often be the first step on the path to success.（形式主语合并）

- 杭女士向我讲述了一个令人鼓舞的故事。她在互联网上筛选出她认为需要帮助的学生，并提供奖学金帮助他们。

  Ms. Hang told us an inspiring story of **how** she had established scholarships by identifying students in need of assistance on the Internet.（宾语从句合并）

- 他的女儿们对他心存感激，因为他为了她们和她们的未来牺牲了这么多，这么努力地工作。

  His daughters are very grateful to him, **for** he has sacrificed so much and worked so hard for them and their future.（原因状语从句合并）

- 1992 年，邓小平在中国南方视察了上海、武汉和深圳等地。其间他发表了关于中国经济由计划经济转向市场经济的几个重要讲话。

  In 1992, Deng Xiaoping had undertaken a very important tour of

China's south visiting cities like Shanghai, Wuhan, and Shenzhen **during which** he made several speeches about China moving from a planned economy to a market economy.（定语从句合并）

7.1.2 并列句拆分与合并

英语的并列句由两个或多个相互有关联的简单句加上并列连词构成。并列连词根据其逻辑关系，可以分为并列关系，如 and、both…and、as well as、not only…but (also)、neither…nor 等；转折关系，如 but、however、yet、still、while 等；选择关系，如 or、either…or、not…but、or else 等；因果关系，如 for、so、so that、because、therefore、thus 等。在英译汉时，根据需要从并列连词处拆译成汉语的简单句；反之，在汉译英时，可以用并列连词把汉语句子合并成英语的并列句。例如：

英译汉

- I have never written a job description for a driver, **but** the one who picked us up from Shanghai Pudong Airport would seem to me a perfect representation of the best qualities needed for the role: punctual, patient, pleasant, helpful, and calm.

  我从未描述过司机的工作，但这位来上海浦东机场接我们的司机是个例外。对我来说，他具备了一个司机应有的最好品质：耐心守时，令人愉悦，乐于助人，沉着冷静。（转折连词处拆分）

- Shanghai literally means "upon the sea" **and** Shanghai is now indeed the largest container port in the world.

  上海在字面上的意思是：在大海上。现在上海也确实是世界上最大的集装箱港口。（并列连词处拆分）

- The new approach also makes sure that any development is never at the expense of our heritage—planning for Westminster must be about today's conservation and building tomorrow's heritage.

  新办法也确保任何开发都不会以牺牲我们的遗产为代价。为威斯

第七章　句子口译技巧

敏斯特市做规划必须要保护今日的文化遗产，并建设明日的文化遗产。（并列处拆分）

- I admit that different political views will make people drift away, **but** from my personal experience I gradually realized that culture connects people.

  我承认政见不同会让人渐行渐远，但我从个人经历中渐渐意识到文化把人们联系在一起。（转折连词处拆分）

- I love Chinese culture—food and drink, music, art, movies, opera, sports, architecture, fashion and dance, perhaps **because** I don't need to be able to say Chinese to appreciate Chinese culture.

  我热爱中国文化——美酒佳肴、音乐绘画、影视歌剧、体育运动、建筑、时尚和舞蹈，也许是因为我不必说中文就能欣赏中国文化吧。（因果连词处拆分）

汉译英

- 中国是一个多民族国家，有56个民族，通用语为汉语。

  China is a multi-ethnic country with 56 ethnic groups, **and** Chinese is the common-used language.（加并列连词合并）

- 她说：过去的"中国制造"意味着廉价，就像50年前的"日本制造"一样。她希望将来的"中国制造"成为品质和领先科技的标志。

  She says that today "Made in China" means cheap, just like "Made in Japan" 50 years ago, **but** her hope is that in the future "Made in China" will become a badge of quality and leading technology.（加转折连词合并）

- 中国的发展离不开世界，世界的发展也离不开中国。

  China cannot develop itself in isolation from the world, **and** vice versa.（加并列连词合并）

- 大家都笑了起来。你看，幽默和笑声也是一种文化联结。

We laughed, **because** humor and laughter are a cultural connection.（加因果连词合并）

- 那年他竞选副市长没有成功。那一次失利成为他生活的一个转折点。

    He was not successful in his election as Deputy Mayor, **but** that failure was a turning point of his life.（加转折连词合并）

7.1.3 谓语、非谓语动词拆分与合并

在英译汉时，可以把英语的并列谓语拆译成汉语的短句，或在非谓语动词不定式、动名词、分词处拆译成汉语的短句；反之，在汉译英时，可以用上述方法进行合并。例如：

英译汉

- The plan puts issues that matter most to local people at the heart of it, **delivering** affordable homes, a world-leading business environment, and more green spaces.

    该计划把最事关当地人的问题作为核心。它旨在为人们提供可负担的住房、世界一流的商业环境和更多的绿地。（现在分词处拆分）

- At the end of the year, I'd like to ask you to raise your glasses **to** toast to our health and a prosperous New Year! Cheers!

    在这年终岁末之际，我请大家和我一起举杯，为健康干杯，为新的一年繁荣昌盛干杯！（不定式处拆分）

- **Sharing** a common passion for climbing with his parents, Tom had already climbed some of the world's most challenging peaks in his professional climbing career.

    汤姆和他父母一样热爱登山。在他的专业登山生涯里，他已经攀登过一些世界上最具挑战性的山峰。（现在分词处拆分）

- It has turned the world into a global village **and made** the international community become a highly interdependent community of a shared future for mankind.

它将世界变成了一个地球村，并使国际社会成为一个高度相互依存的命运共同体。（并列谓语处拆分）

- It is therefore an honor for me to welcome you to the ancient Guildhall in the City of London for a conference **intended** both to examine and to strengthen the relationship between Britain and China.

因此，我很荣幸地欢迎您到伦敦金融城古老的市政厅参加会议。此次会议旨在讨论和加强英中关系。（过去分词处拆分）

汉译英

- 我们应该总结和利用两国友好合作经验，更好造福两国人民。

We should sum up and take full advantage of the experience we have gained in our friendly cooperation **so as to** bring more benefits to our two peoples.（加不定式合并）

- 中英关系"黄金时代"的战略定位更加清晰，双方政治互信进一步加强，合作内涵更加充实。

China and the U.K. reconfirmed the strategic definition of the "Golden Era", enhanced political trust, **and enriched** bilateral cooperation.（加并列谓语合并）

- 中华人民共和国，简称"中国"，是世界文明古国之一。

The People's Republic of China **known** as China for short is one of the oldest civilizations in the world.（加过去分词合并）

- 我们希望英方坚持开放包容，排除各种干扰，为华为等在英中国企业营造公平、透明、非歧视的营商环境。

It is our hope that the U.K. will remain open and inclusive, resist disruptions, **and continue** to foster a fair, transparent, and non-discriminatory business environment for Huawei and other Chinese companies in the U.K.（加并列谓语合并）

- 以人为本、造福于民，不仅是中英两国发展的目标，也是中英关系发展的基石。

  In China-U.K. relations, **putting** the people first and **working** for the many is not only the goal but also the foundation.（加动名词合并）

7.1.4 短语拆分与合并

在英译汉时，可以把独立主格、同位语、名词短语和介词短语等拆分成一个单独的句子；反之，在汉译英时，可以利用上述结构进行合并。例如：

英译汉

- The conference is our flagship event, with **each installment addressing** one of the great themes of the day, such as the relationship between China and Britain.

  这个会议是我们的旗舰活动，每一次会议都会针对当今的一个重大主题，如中英关系这个主题。（独立主格处拆分）

- We hope to both explore and build on the relationship between Britain and China, **one that** is already of vital importance, and can only grow more significant.

  我们希望探索和加强英中关系。两国关系现已经非常重要，而且这种关系只会变得愈加重要。（同位语处拆分）

- Her mother and father, **academics who** do research on mathematics at Oxford University, would also take the family on holidays to the countryside.

  她的父母是牛津大学研究数学的学者，他们也会带着家人去农村度假。（同位语处拆分）

- We've got Reading Rooms for research and study, exhibitions, and events, and **plenty of great places** to eat, drink, and shop.

我们有阅读室用于研究和学习、举行展览以及组织活动。我们还有许多好地方可以吃饭、喝酒和购物。（名词短语处拆分）

- He applied the life skills **of** hard work, being positive even when the odds are against him, perseverance, and building successful teams in the commercial world, which he had learned in the military.

  他把在部队中学到的生存技能运用到了商业领域中，那就是艰苦奋斗、遇到困难时要积极向上、坚持不懈和组建成功团队。（介词短语处拆分）

汉译英

- 双方合作成果丰硕，2018年中英贸易额首次突破800亿美元大关，其中英国对华出口同比增长6.9%。

  Fruitful results have been achieved with **China-U.K. bilateral trade in 2018 exceeding** 80 billion dollars for the first time and **U.K. exports to China increasing** by 6.9%.（加独立主格合并）

- 我在伦敦希思罗机场4号航站楼等待飞往上海的航班，之后将转飞北京，开启我们2018年的徒步之旅。

  I am in Heathrow Terminal 4 waiting to board my flight to Shanghai and then up to Beijing, **the start of our 2018 walk**.（加同位语合并）

- 他们道别后，一个回了家，一个去了书店。

  They said goodbye to each other, **one to** go home, **the other to** go to the bookstore.（加独立主格合并）

- 我认为在中国一个人能取得成功，除了勤奋、教育和重视家庭等常见因素之外，还有另外一个因素，即个人成就伴随着强烈的社会责任感。

  In addition to the usual ingredients of success in China—hard work, education, and family focus, there is another moral dimension to work—a sense of responsibility to the community born of their personal success.（加介词短语合并）

- 我想借此机会对新闻界的朋友们表示诚挚的感谢，感谢你们对此次会议的辛苦报道。

  I would like to take this opportunity to express my sincere thanks to the friends from the press **for your hard work** in covering the conference.（加介词短语合并）

英汉句子的拆分与合并并不局限于单一的方法，有时会多种方法并用。例如：

英译汉

- So, let us, in the next five days, start a long march together, **not in lockstep**, but on different roads leading to the same goal, **the goal of building** a world structure of peace and justice **in which** all may stand together with equal dignity and **in which** each nation, large or small, has a right to determine its own form of government, free of outside interference or domination.

  所以，让我们在随后的五天里，开始一个长征吧！不是亦步亦趋，而是从不同的道路走向同一个目标。这个目标就是建立一个和平和正义的世界格局。在此格局下，每个人都享有同等的尊严，每个国家，无论大小，都有权决定自己的政府形式，不受外来的干涉和控制。（介词短语、同位语、定语从句处拆分）

- His efforts **were rewarded with** incredible financial success **though** he overlooks this **and is** most proud of the 2,000 good jobs he has created.

  他的努力获得了巨大的经济回报。但是他不看重这一点，他更为自豪的是自己创造了 2 000 个良好的就业机会。（利用介词短语、并列句、并列谓语合并）

汉译英

- 五年前，习近平主席提出"一带一路"倡议，宗旨是促进各国各地区互联互通，形成联动发展的新格局，为世界经济增长拓展新空间。

第七章 句子口译技巧

The Belt and Road Initiative **proposed** by President Xi Jinping five years ago is aimed at **enhancing** connectivity between countries and regions of the world **so as to** achieve interconnected development and open new space for world's economic growth. （利用过去分词作定语、动名词作宾语、不定式作目的状语合并）

- 中国是世界上最大的发展中国家，社会生产力水平总体还比较低，还需要经过几十年的艰苦奋斗才能实现现代化。我们需要长期和平的国际环境，尤其是长期的睦邻友好环境。

As the largest developing country in the world **with** a relatively low level of productivity on the whole, China needs a long-term peaceful international environment and a good neighborly environment in particular **to** realize its modernization program through decades of arduous struggles. （利用状语从句、介词短语、不定式作目的状语合并）

> 技巧训练：用拆分法口译下列句子。

练习一　视译

1）Economic globalization, as the trend of the times, should not and cannot be held back.

2）Both Britain and China today are dynamic, modern world economies, working together to promote even closer political, cultural, and trade ties.

3）While China opens wider to the U.S. and the rest of the world, we expect the U.S. to do the same to China and remove all unreasonable restrictions.

4）All these point to one simple fact: Cooperation benefits both China and the United States and the rest of the world, and friction will only create a lose-lose situation and harm the whole world.

5）I am confident that when we effectively enhance mutual trust, properly manage differences, and strengthen exchanges and cooperation in keeping with the principle of no conflict or confrontation, mutual respect, and win-win cooperation, China-U.S. relations will surely enjoy sound and steady growth, bringing greater benefits to people of our two countries and beyond.

6）长城是中国古代的伟大建筑工程之一，始建于2 000多年前，全长8 851公里，号称"万里长城"。

7）长江全长6 387公里，是中国第一大河流，世界第三大河流。

8）黄河流经中国的9个省和自治区，全长5 464公里，流域面积为752 443平方公里。

9）中国陆地面积居世界第三位，约占世界陆地面积的十五分之一。

10）中国是一个大国，有五分之四的人口从事农业，但耕地只占土地面积的十分之一，其余为山脉、森林、城镇用地和其他用地。

练习二　听译（1—10）

7.2　词类转换技巧

　　英语的语言特征是以静态为主，多用名词，名词化表意现象极为普遍；同时，英语中大量使用介词、形容词（作表语）和副词等。汉语多使用动词，形成了以动态为主的语言特征。由于英语和汉语在语法和习惯表达上的差异，在保持原文意思不变的情况下，译文必须改变词类或句子成分，以顺应各自语言表达的需要，这种转换技巧被称为词类转换法。在英译汉时，可以将英语中的名词、副词、介词或形容词转换成汉语的动词；反之，在汉译英时，则需要把汉语的动词相应地转换成英语的名词、副词、介词或形容词等。词类转换法是英汉互译中经常使用的方法。下文将从英语名词、副词、介词、形容词转换为汉语动词方面进行具体阐释。

7.2.1 英语名词转换为汉语动词

在英译汉中,最重要、最常见的词类转换是名词与动词之间的互相转换。能转换成汉语动词的英语名词主要有四类:由动词派生形成的英语名词;具有动作意味的英语名词;以 -er 结尾表示身份或职业的英语名词;作为习语主体的英语名词。例如:

- Experts say the research is another piece of **evidence** that physical exercise can help protect a person's health.

  专家认为这项研究又一次证明体育锻炼有助于保持身体健康。

- Too much **exposure** to TV programs will do great harm to the eyesight of children.

  孩子们看电视过多会极大地损害视力。

- The kids were better **skiers** when they were three year olds than I am now.

  孩子们三岁时滑雪就比我现在滑得要好。

- We place the high **value** on our friendly relations with developing countries.

  我们高度重视与发展中国家的友好关系。

- Today's rapid development in science and technology is bringing about increasingly great **impact** on global political and economic pattern and people's social life.

  当今科学技术的突飞猛进,越来越深刻地影响着世界的政治经济格局和人们的社会生活。

7.2.2 英语副词转换为汉语动词

在英语句子中,作表语或宾语补足语的副词有时可以译成汉语动词,这类英语副词常见的有 in、out、over 等。例如:

- When I look for Mr. Ren, he was **out**.

  当我找任先生时,他<u>出去了</u>。

- He won't go out having his supper, if the game is not **over**.

  只要游戏没有<u>结束</u>,他就不出来吃晚饭。

- Application must be **in** by April 30.

  申请务必于 4 月 30 日之前<u>寄到</u>。

- What's **on** at the cinema?

  电影院正在<u>上映</u>什么电影?

- I wasn't **in** when you rang me up.

  当你给我打电话时,我不<u>在</u>。

7.2.3 英语介词转换为汉语动词

在英语句子中,当介词或介词短语作表语或状语时,或者当介词具有动作意义时,可以将其转换成汉语的动词。例如:

- When I came into the room, I found him **at** books.

  当我走进房间时,他正在<u>看</u>书。

- She has been **on** the computer since this morning.

  从早晨到现在,她一直在<u>玩</u>电脑。

- The plane crushed **out of** control.

  这架飞机因<u>失去</u>控制而坠毁。

- In the summer, we have a rainy season **for** three weeks.

  在夏天,雨季要<u>持续</u>三周。

- I did not eat much at the buffet, because I am **on a diet**.

  我没有吃多少自助餐,因为我正在<u>减肥</u>。

第七章　句子口译技巧

7.2.4 英语形容词转换为汉语动词

当英语中表示知觉、情感、欲望等心理状态的形容词作表语时，可以将其转换成汉语的动词。例如：

- The apartment is near the sea. I'm **sure** you will like it.

  公寓离海边很近，我相信您一定会喜欢的。

- He was **convinced** that a bright future is waiting for him.

  他确信自己会有一个美好的未来。

- I'm very **grateful** for what you have done for us since we set foot on this land.

  非常感谢到贵国后你们为我们所做的一切。

- He was **concerned** with the enhancement of the human condition.

  他关心人类生存环境的改善。

- I feel **certain** that it will all turn out well.

  我肯定一切都会皆大欢喜的。

> 技巧训练：用词类转换法口译下列句子。

练习三　视译

1) After more than one year of preparation and with the strong support from various parties, the exhibition is officially opened.

2) We are delighted by the warmth of the welcome which you have given us.

3) We look forward to seeing the dignity of your Northern Capital; the vigor of Shanghai in the east; the magnificence of the ancient Terracotta Warriors; Kunming—the city of eternal spring in the west; and Guangzhou, looking out to the South Sea China.

4) We also welcome the opportunity to see what you are achieving now, and

meet some of the people behind those achievements.

5）We are ready and believe in ourselves that we can contribute to the realization of China's plans for the future.

6）感谢你们对我们的热烈欢迎，今天的晚餐对我们来说尤其难忘。

7）把更多的可能变为现实，关键是要营造良好的环境。

8）这是一个很好的例子，说明了我们两国之间的良好关系在实践中的意义。

9）有就业就有收入，就能带来新的消费和投资，从而推动经济发展良性循环。

10）人类社会要持续进步，各国就应该坚持要开放不要封闭，要合作不要对抗，要共赢不要独占。

练习四　听译（1—10）

7.3 环境保护口译

7.3.1 环境保护译前准备

A. 词汇

- 生物圈：biosphere
- 生态系统：ecosystem
- 生物多样性：biodiversity
- 自然资源：natural resources
- 自然保护区：nature reserve
- 全球变暖：global warming
- 气候变化：climate change

- 环境恶化: environmental degradation
- 海洋酸化: ocean acidification
- 生态危机: ecological crisis
- 物种濒危: species endangerment
- 濒危野生动物: endangered wildlife
- 野生动植物: wild fauna and flora
- 人口过剩: overpopulation
- 城市化: urbanization
- 荒漠化: desertification
- 森林砍伐: deforestation
- 过度开发: over-exploitation
- 水土流失: water and soil erosion
- 风/沙尘暴: wind/sand breaks
- 土壤碱化: soil alkalization
- 农药残留: pesticide residue
- 污染: pollution
- 温室气体排放: greenhouse gas emissions
- 温室效应: greenhouse effect
- 二氧化碳: carbon dioxide (CO_2)
- 矿物燃料: fossil fuel
- 悬浮颗粒物: suspended particles
- 工业粉尘排放: industrial dust discharged
- 工业废弃物: industrial solid wastes
- 白色污染: white pollution
- 环保农业/生态农业: environmental-friendly agriculture / eco-agriculture
- 绿化区: afforested areas / greening space

- 绿化工程: afforestation project
- 大气监测系统: atmospheric monitoring system
- 垃圾分类: garbage sorting
- 厨房垃圾/可回收垃圾/不可回收垃圾: kitchen garbage / recoverable garbage / unrecoverable garbage
- 自然资源的过度消耗: over-consumption of natural resources
- 对水和空气质量的影响: impact on the quality of water and air
- 遏制环境污染: curb environmental pollution / bring the pollution under control
- 坚持环境保护基本国策: adhere to the basic state policy of environmental protection
- 推行可持续发展战略: pursue the strategy of sustainable development
- 提高全民环保意识: raise environmental awareness amongst the general public
- 查处违反环保法规案件: investigate and punish acts of violating laws and regulations on environmental protection
- 联合国环境规划署: United Nations Environment Programs (UNEP)
- 联合国环境与发展大会(环发大会): United Nations Conference on Environment and Development (UNCED)
- 《联合国防治荒漠化国际公约》: United Nations Convention to Combat Desertification (UNCCD)
- 《联合国生物多样性公约》: United Nations Convention on Biological Diversity (UNCBD)
- 全民义务植树日: National Tree-Planting Day
- 中国生物多样性保护行动计划: China Biological Diversity Protection Action Plan
- 中国跨世纪绿色工程规划: China Trans-Century Green Project Plan

- 中华人民共和国自然资源部: Ministry of Natural Resources, PRC
- 中华人民共和国生态环境部: Ministry of Ecology and Environment, PRC

B. 背景知识

- 《联合国气候变化框架公约》: United Nations Framework Convention on Climate Change (UNFCCC)

  It is an international environmental treaty adopted on May 9, 1992 and then entered into force on March 21, 1994. Its objective is to "stabilize greenhouse gas concentrations in the atmosphere at a level that would prevent dangerous anthropogenic interference with the climate system".

- 《巴黎协定》: Paris Agreement

  The Paris Agreement, signed in 2016, is an agreement within UNFCCC, dealing with greenhouse-gas-emission mitigation, adaptation, and finance. Under the Agreement, each country must determine, plan, and regularly report on the contribution that it undertakes to mitigate global warming. Its long-term temperature goal is to keep the increase in global average temperature to well below 2℃ above pre-industrial levels; and to pursue efforts to limit the increase to 1.5℃, recognizing that this would substantially reduce the risks and impacts of climate change. It also aims to increase the ability of parties to adapt to the adverse impacts of climate change, and make "finance flows consistent with a pathway towards low greenhouse gas emissions and climate-resilient development".

- 环境恶化: environmental degradation

  Environmental degradation is the deterioration of the environment through depletion of resources such as air, water, and soil; the destruction of ecosystems; habitat destruction; the extinction of wildlife; and pollution. It is defined as any change or disturbance to the environment perceived to be deleterious or undesirable.

- 可再生能源: renewable energy

  Renewable energy is the energy that is collected from renewable resources, which are naturally replenished on a human timescale, such as sunlight, wind, rain, tides, waves, and geothermal heat. Renewable energy often provides energy in four important areas: electricity generation, air and water heating/cooling, transportation, and rural (off-grid) energy services.

- 世界环境日: World Environment Day

  World Environment Day is the United Nations' campaign for encouraging worldwide awareness and action for the environment. Over the years, it has grown to be a global platform for public outreach that is widely celebrated by stakeholders in over 100 countries. It also serves as the people's day for doing something positive for the environment, inspiring individual actions, and galvanizing them into a collective power that generates an exponential positive impact on the planet. Its celebrations culminate on June 5 every year.

- 《中华人民共和国环境保护法》: Environmental Protection Law of the People's Republic of China

  It is a national law formulated for the purpose of protecting and improving environment, preventing and controlling pollution and other public hazards, safeguarding public health, promoting ecological civilization improvement, and facilitating sustainable economic and social development.

- 世界园艺博览会: International Horticultural Expos

  It is a type of international exhibition held under the joint auspices of the BIE (Bureau International des Exhibitions, 国际展览局) and the AIPH (International Association of Horticultural Producers, 国际园艺生产者协会). Its events can last a minimum of 3 months and a maximum of 6 months, and can take place every 2 years in different countries and once a decade in the same country. China has hosted the 1999 Kunming World Horticultural Exposition with the theme of "Man and Nature—Marching into the 21st Century" and International Horticultural Exhibition 2019 Beijing with the theme of "Live Green, Live Better".

The international exposition aims at promoting the exchanges, cooperation, and development in the fields of economy, culture, science, and technology of all countries in the world, exhibits the latest achievements of each country in various fields, and promotes the international trade and technological cooperation. It also promotes the urban construction and development of the host cities. Since the international exposition is of large scale, high level, and distinct representative, it is also called the "Olympics of the World Economy, Culture, Science, and Technology".

7.3.2 环境保护连续口译

课堂练习：口译下列语段，注意句子的拆分、合并，以及词类转换。

练习五　视译

1) Every day, millions of us climb into our cars and set off on journeys to work, to the shops, or to travel. Few of us in the car think about the environmental impact of driving in heavy traffic. The carbon dioxide emitted by the burning of diesel and gasoline from different vehicles is the main source of the rapidly increasing greenhouse gas pollution. Therefore, the costs of our car-dependent lifestyles are becoming increasingly serious. The lengthening

traffic jams, demands for new roads, increasing air pollution, and the threat of climate change are all issues we must tackle sooner rather than later.

2) As the world is undergoing profound changes unseen in a century and the Fourth Industrial Revolution unfolds, there has been an important reform in energy production and consumption. In face of global challenges such as climate change, new and renewable energy is replacing fossil fuel, and green, low-carbon, and sustainable growth has become the major trend in global development. We need to focus more on the quality of economic growth, so as to make a contribution to sustainable development and the global efforts against climate change.

3) 当前，保护环境是一项基本国策。中国政府高度重视生态环境保护和建设，采取了一系列战略措施，并加大了环境保护力度。秉承尊重自然、顺应自然、保护自然的理念，中国将实施资源节约和环境保护的基本国策，更加自觉地促进绿色发展、循环发展和低碳发展，将生态文明建设与经济、政治、文化和社会建设全方位和全过程配套发展。

4) 中国已采取各种措施应对环境问题，比如鼓励人们进行垃圾分类，以便回收和再利用。十年前，为了遏制塑料袋造成的"白色污染"和能源浪费，国务院办公厅规定所有的超市、商场、集贸市场等场所一律不得免费提供塑料购物袋，并在全国范围内禁止生产、销售和使用厚度小于0.025毫米的塑料袋。2013年，中国开始推行"绿篱"行动，大幅限制从其他国家进口废弃物。在创新、协调、绿色、开放和共享发展的理念指导下，中国正在加快清洁和可再生能源的开发和利用，比如水能、风能、太阳能和生物质能。

练习六　听译（1—4）

第七章　句子口译技巧

> 小组练习：五人一组，每人依次读一个自然段，其他人轮流进行连续口译。口译结束后，小组进行讨论，挑选十个典型句子进行拆分翻译，并将英汉翻译对照文本上交。

练习七

A Joint Response to Climate Change, a Better Environment for Our Planet [1]

UN Headquarters; September 23, 2019

Your Excellency Secretary-General Antonio Guterres,

Your Excellencies Heads of State and Government,

Ladies and gentlemen,

China highly commends and supports the Secretary-General's initiative for convening this Summit.

Climate change is a common challenge to all countries. To jointly tackle this challenge and protect the planet we all call home will be a journey critical to the future and destiny of humankind.

As global climate governance enters a crucial stage, the international community must stick to the right approach, that is, making a joint response to climate change with unwavering commitment and unrelenting efforts. In tackling climate change, we must:

First, be determined to win the fight. We must honor our commitments, follow through on the Paris Agreement and its implementation guidelines, and see to it that both this Summit and the COP25 produce positive outcomes that will inject fresh impetus into the post-2020 multilateral process. The withdrawal of certain parties will not shake the collective will of the international community,

---

1　Extracts from Remarks by Wang Yi, Special Representative of President Xi Jinping, State Councilor and Minister of Foreign Affairs at the UN Climate Action Summit.

nor will it possibly reverse the historical trend of international cooperation.

Second, be prepared to take sustained actions. A response to climate change does not have to be made at the expense of development. We must make sure that our climate actions are mutually reinforcing with our socioeconomic endeavors, realize a transformation towards green and low-carbon development, and enhance climate resilience in the process of accelerating development. We must mobilize stakeholders and resources across all sectors to scale up pre-2020 to avoid passing on the responsibilities to the post-2020 process.

Third, be committed to cooperation. The joint fight against climate change requires us to uphold multilateralism and explore solutions within the framework of the UNFCCC and the Paris Agreement. In particular, it is important that we follow the principles of "common but differentiated responsibilities", equity, and respective capabilities, respect the need for development and the special conditions of developing countries, and help them build preparedness. Developed countries, on their part, need to take the lead in reducing emissions and honor their commitment of mobilizing $100 billion a year in climate finance by 2020.

As a responsible member of the international community, China honors its words and keeps taking actions on climate change.

Guided by a philosophy of innovative, coordinated, green, open, and shared development, China is pursuing high-quality growth and following a path of green, low-carbon, and sustainable development. China will faithfully fulfill our obligations under the UNFCCC and the Paris Agreement, and realize as scheduled its nationally determined contribution targets submitted to the UNFCCC secretariat.

We will continue to promote joint building of a green Belt and Road. We are implementing the Belt and Road South-South Cooperation Initiative on Climate Change, and mobilizing stronger support for international cooperation against climate change through the BRI International Green Development

第七章 句子口译技巧

Coalition and other platforms.

Nature-Based Solutions (NBS) is one of the nine action tracks of this Summit. China is honored to co-lead this track with New Zealand at the invitation of the Secretary-General. Through collaborating with many other countries and international organizations in this area, we gained fruitful results in the following aspects.

First, a deeper insight into the relations between man and nature. Human beings and nature are inseparable. We need to respect, adapt to, and protect nature. NBS advocates the harmonious co-existence between man and nature, values ecological progress, and incorporates the sustainable use of natural resources into climate policies and action frameworks, thus leveraging the role of nature to the fullest extent possible in enhancing the effectiveness of climate actions.

Second, new measures for the global fight against climate change. We have proposed over 150 initiatives in such areas as forestry, agriculture, ocean, water resources, and the systemic role of nature, and set up a Group of Friends for NBS mechanism for follow-ups to keep up the momentum of international cooperation in these areas. Our goal is to achieve nature's mitigation potential of cutting 10 to 12 gigatons of CO_2 per year.

Third, fresh support for the Sustainable Development Goals. The Chinese often say that green is as precious as gold. In other words, a better environment can bring about greater productivity. We have collected over 30 best practices in forest carbon sink, bio-diversity protection, and desertification prevention and treatment to demonstrate how NBS can significantly promote coordinated economic, social, and environmental development. I believe that those best practices will provide useful references for countries to better implement the 2030 Agenda for Sustainable Development.

Long and difficult as the journey of tackling climate change is, sustained actions will take us to the destination. No matter how the international landscape may evolve, there will be no change in China's efforts to fight against climate change, its readiness to deepen climate cooperation with other countries, or its commitment to the multilateral process on climate change. I am convinced that by working together as one and in the same direction, we will build a clean and beautiful world where we enjoy shared prosperity and shared future.

Thank you.

练习八

共谋绿色生活，共建美丽家园[1]

尊敬的各位国家元首，政府首脑和夫人，

尊敬的国际展览局秘书长和国际园艺生产者协会主席，

尊敬的各国使节，各位国际组织代表，

女士们，先生们，朋友们：

"迟日江山丽，春风花草香。"四月的北京，春回大地，万物复苏。很高兴同各位嘉宾相聚在雄伟的长城脚下、美丽的妫水河畔，共同拉开2019年中国北京世界园艺博览会大幕。

首先，我谨代表中国政府和中国人民，并以我个人的名义，对远道而来的各位嘉宾，表示热烈的欢迎！对支持和参与北京世界园艺博览会的各国朋友，表示衷心的感谢！

北京世界园艺博览会以"绿色生活，美丽家园"为主题，旨在倡导人们尊重自然、融入自然、追求美好生活。北京世界园艺博览会园区，同大自然的湖光山色交相辉映。我希望，这片园区所阐释的绿色发展理念能传达至世界各个角落。

锦绣中华大地，是中华民族赖以生存和发展的家园，孕育了中华民族5 000多年的灿烂文明，造就了中华民族天人合一的崇高追求。

现在，生态文明建设已经纳入中国国家发展总体布局，建设美丽中国已经成为中国人民心向往之的奋斗目标。中国生态文明建设进入了快

---

[1] 2019年4月28日，中国国家主席习近平在中国北京世界园艺博览会开幕式上的讲话。来自新华网网站。

车道,天更蓝、山更绿、水更清将不断展现在世人面前。

纵观人类文明发展史,生态兴则文明兴,生态衰则文明衰。工业化进程创造了前所未有的物质财富,也产生了难以弥补的生态创伤。杀鸡取卵、竭泽而渔的发展方式走到了尽头,顺应自然、保护生态的绿色发展昭示着未来。

仰望夜空,繁星闪烁。地球是全人类赖以生存的唯一家园。我们要像保护自己的眼睛一样保护生态环境,像对待生命一样对待生态环境,同筑生态文明之基,同走绿色发展之路!

我们应该追求人与自然和谐。山峦层林尽染,平原蓝绿交融,城乡鸟语花香。这样的自然美景,既带给人们美的享受,也是人类走向未来的依托。无序开发、粗暴掠夺,人类定会遭到大自然的无情报复;合理利用、友好保护,人类必将获得大自然的慷慨回报。我们要维持地球生态整体平衡,让子孙后代既能享有丰富的物质财富,又能遥望星空、看见青山、闻到花香。

我们应该追求绿色发展繁荣。绿色是大自然的底色。我一直讲,绿水青山就是金山银山,改善生态环境就是发展生产力。良好生态本身蕴含着无穷的经济价值,能够源源不断创造综合效益,实现经济社会可持续发展。

我们应该追求热爱自然情怀。"取之有度,用之有节",是生态文明的真谛。我们要倡导简约适度、绿色低碳的生活方式,拒绝奢华和浪费,形成文明健康的生活风尚。要倡导环保意识、生态意识,构建全社会共同参与的环境治理体系,让生态环保思想成为社会生活中的主流文化。要倡导尊重自然、爱护自然的绿色价值观念,让天蓝地绿水清深入人心,形成深刻的人文情怀。

我们应该追求科学治理精神。生态治理必须遵循规律,科学规划,因地制宜,统筹兼顾,打造多元共生的生态系统。只有赋之以人类智慧,地球家园才会充满生机活力。生态治理,道阻且长,行则将至。我们既要有只争朝夕的精神,更要有持之以恒的坚守。

我们应该追求携手合作应对。建设美丽家园是人类的共同梦想。面对生态环境挑战，人类是一荣俱荣、一损俱损的命运共同体，没有哪个国家能独善其身。唯有携手合作，我们才能有效应对气候变化、海洋污染、生物保护等全球性环境问题，实现联合国2030年可持续发展目标。只有并肩同行，才能让绿色发展理念深入人心、全球生态文明之路行稳致远。

昨天，第二届"一带一路"国际合作高峰论坛成功闭幕，在座许多嘉宾出席了论坛。共建"一带一路"就是要建设一条开放发展之路，同时也必须是一条绿色发展之路。这是与会各方达成的重要共识。中国愿同各国一道，共同建设美丽地球家园，共同构建人类命运共同体。

一代人有一代人的使命。建设生态文明，功在当代，利在千秋。让我们从自己、从现在做起，把接力棒一棒一棒传下去。

我宣布，2019年中国北京世界园艺博览会开幕！

第八章 数字口译

数字口译对初学者而言是一个极大的挑战,一是因为英汉数字的计数单位存在很大差异,万以上的数字单位不能直接对译,必须进行相应的转换;二是因为数字之间没有内在的逻辑,很难记忆。无论译员的记忆力有多好,他都不可能记住所有数字,特别是大的数字。数字口译在很大程度上依赖于译员的瞬时处理能力,一旦疏忽,就可能会丢失数字信息。巧妙地记数字可以帮助译员缩短英汉数字互译的时间,避免出现误译,进而达到较好的口译效果。

8.1 基本数字口译

8.1.1 基数词与序数词

基数词(cardinal numbers)表示数量,如汉语中的一、二、三、四、五等,阿拉伯数字中的1、2、3、4、5等,英语中的one、two、three、four、five等。序数词(ordinal numbers)表示顺序,如汉语中的第一、第二、第三、第四、第五等,英语中的first、second、third、fourth、fifth等。汉语的序数词除了在基数词前面加"第"之外,数字没有形式上的变化,而英语的序数词相比于基数词却发生了变化。具体见表8-1:

表 8–1　英语基数词与序数词对照表

基数词	英语表述	序数词	英语表述
1	one	1st	first
2	two	2nd	second
3	three	3rd	third
4	four	4th	fourth
5	five	5th	fifth
9	nine	9th	ninth
12	twelve	12th	twelfth
13	thirteen	13th	thirteenth
20	twenty	20th	twentieth
21	twenty one	21st	twenty-first
100	one hundred	100th	hundredth
1000	one thousand	1000th	thousandth

技巧训练：口译下列句子。

练习一

1) Chinese investment in the U.K. ranks the first, ahead of investments in other European countries.
2) China is the second largest economy in the world.
3) 2019 marks the 70th anniversary of the founding of the People's Republic of China.
4) The 15th day of the first Lunar month is China's Lantern Festival.
5) A new system is needed to meet the speed and complexity of a 21st-century global economy.

8.1.2 百分数、小数与分数

百分数（percentage）、小数（decimal）与分数（fraction）可以表示同一数值，因写法、读法各不相同，译员应熟练掌握。具体见表 8–2：

表 8–2 常用百分数、小数与分数对照表

百分数	小数	分数	分数英语表述
1%	0.01	1/100	one a hundredth
5%	0.05	1/20	one twentieth
10%	0.1	1/10	one tenth
12.5%	0.125	1/8	one eighth
20%	0.2	1/5	one fifth
25%	0.25	1/4	a quarter
33%	0.33	1/3	a third
50%	0.5	1/2	a half
75%	0.75	3/4	three quarters/three fourths
80%	0.8	4/5	four fifths
90%	0.9	9/10	nine tenths
99%	0.99	99/100	ninety-nine over a hundred
100%	1	—	—
125%	1.25	$1\frac{1}{4}$	one and a quarter
150%	1.5	$1\frac{1}{2}$	one and a half
200%	2	—	—

> 技巧训练：口译下列句子。

练习二

1) China is a developing country with the biggest population in the world. A sample survey shows that China's population had reached 1.415 billion by the end of 2018, accounting for about 18.54% of the world's population.

2) In 2019, the unemployment rate in China came in at between 5% and 5.3% and remained stable throughout the year.

3) China is home to two thirds of the world's self-made female billionaires.

4) More than a quarter of Americans now have university degrees, according to a new research.

5) Wealth in Great Britain is unequally divided. The richest 10% of households hold 45% of all wealth. The poorest 50%, by contrast, own just 8.7%.

8.1.3 比率

比率（rates/ratios）是两个或多个数的比值。比率有时可以表示为分数或小数。例如：

- The ratio of men's jobs to women's is 8 to 1 (8:1).
- Salad dressing may be made using the ratio 1:2 by volume of vinegar to oil (one part vinegar to two parts oil).
- A mixture contains 200 ml of milk and 500 ml of water. The ratio of milk to water is 2:5.

速率、费率等是一种特殊的比率。它是单位分母为 1 的测量比值。例如：

- Paul travels at an average speed of 60 kilometers per hour (60 kph) over a period of two hours.

- England has become the most crowded nation in Europe, with 395 people per square kilometer.
- We can offer you forty days' holiday per annum.

> 技巧训练：口译下列句子。

练习三

1) England was knocked out of the 2018 Football World Cup after losing 1:2 to the Croatian team in the semi-finals.
2) The ideal teacher to student ratio in a school is anywhere between 1:10 to 1:40.
3) The average person types between 38 and 40 words per minute (WPM); however, professional typists type a lot faster—on average between 65 and 75 WPM.
4) Workers in this country aged 16 or over are legally entitled to a minimum wage of £7.83 per hour.
5) If a business charges its customers 1.5% per month on any unpaid balance, the per annum rate is 18%.

8.1.4 倍数

英汉两种语言在倍数（multiples）增减的表达上存在很大差异。英语的倍数表达都包括基数；汉语的倍数表达有一些句式包括基数，有一些句式不包括基数。根据下列例句，试比较英汉倍数表达的异同：

- This desk is twice as long as that one.
- This desk is twice longer than that one.
- This desk is twice the length of that one.

这三个英文句子均可以表示为：

- 这张桌子是那张桌子的两倍长。（包括基数）
- 这张桌子比那张桌子长一倍。（不包括基数）

又如：

- Our salary will double next year.
- Our salary will increase twice next year.

这两个英文句子均可以表示为：

- 我们明年的工资将是现在的两倍。（包括基数）
- 我们明年的工资将增长一倍。（不包括基数）
- 我们明年的工资将翻一番。（不包括基数）

因此，当英语倍数译成汉语倍数时，若用不包括基数的倍数表达，则在原来的倍数上减一；反之，当汉语不包括基数的倍数译成英语倍数时，要在原来的基数上加一。

技巧训练：口译下列句子。

练习四

1) The price of this pen is twice as much as that of the previous one.

2) It's expected that our salary will triple next year.

3) The journey is four times as long as that one. / The journey is four times longer than that one. / The journey is four times the length of that one.

4) This hospital charges five times that of ordinary ones.

5) Compared with 45 years ago when there were only 16 Chinese students in Britain, today, the number has grown to over 160,000. That is an increase by more than 10,000 times.

6) Since the beginning of reform and opening-up, the number of foreign visitors to China has doubled and redoubled.

7）Infant mortality in poor countries is 12 times higher than in rich countries.

8）In the past two decades, we have posted a 14-fold increase in per capita gross domestic product, from about $700 to about $10,000.

8.1.5 不确定数字

不确定数字（indefinite numbers）是指没有确切的数量，表示若干、许多、大量、不少、成千上万等概念的词组。具体见表 8–3：

表 8–3　汉英不确定数字对照表

汉语表述	英语表述
几个	some, a few, several, a number of, a couple…
十几个	more than/over a dozen, less/no more than twenty
数十、几十、好几十、数十年	tens of, dozens of, decades of, scores of
好几百个、数百、数以百计、几百、成百上千	hundreds of
成千上万、数以千计、数万	thousands of
数以百万计的、数百万、几百万、好几百万、千千万万	millions of
数亿、无数	millions upon millions of
数十亿	billions of
大约、大概、左右、将近……	about, around, some, approximately, roughly, close to, nearly, in the neighborhood of, in the region of, more or less, or so, thereabout, toward(s), in the rough…

（续表）

汉语表述	英语表述
超过、多达……	above, more than, over, up to, more…
以下、不足……	below, less than, fewer than, under, within…
从……到、介于……之间……	from…to, between…and…

> 技巧训练：口译下列句子。

练习五

1) The journey took approximately/about/around 7 hours.
2) Millions of people want new, simplified ways of interacting with a computer.
3) Several hundred students gathered on campus.
4) I was meeting these boys who were mostly more or less my own age.
5) The total cost of the project would be more than $240 million.

8.2 大数字口译

8.2.1 汉英数字体系对比

由于英汉的数字表达方式不同，当口译过程中出现大数字时，译员不仅要处理信息，还要进行数字的瞬间转换，这通常会增加口译的难度。所以译员应该熟练掌握阿拉伯数字、汉语数字和英语数字间的转换。具体见表8-4：

第八章 数字口译

表8-4 阿拉伯数字、汉语数字与英语数字对照表

阿拉伯数字	汉语数字	英语数字
1	个	one
10	十	ten
100	百	a hundred
1,000	千	a thousand
10,000	万	ten thousand
100,000	十万	a hundred thousand
1,000,000	百万	a million
10,000,000	千万	ten million
100,000,000	亿	a hundred million
1,000,000,000	十亿	a billion
10,000,000,000	百亿	ten billion
100,000,000,000	千亿	a hundred billion
1,000,000,000,000	万亿	a trillion

从这个对照表可以看出，汉语数字"个""十""百""千""万""十万""百万""千万""亿""十亿""百亿""千亿""万亿"……实际上是"十"的倍数，千以上以"万""亿"为单位。英语数字 one、ten、a hundred、a thousand、ten thousand、a hundred thousand、a million、ten million、a hundred million、a billion、ten billion、a hundred billion、a trillion 等也是十的倍数，千以上以 thousand（千）、million（百万）和 billion（十亿）为单位。这样，汉语数字就形成了三个区间单位，即万以下的区间、万和亿之间的区间以及亿以上的区间。而英语中的 thousand、million、billion 三个单位标尺把数字分成了四个区间单位，即 thousand 以下的区间、thousand 和 million 之间的区间、million 与 billion 之间的区间以及 billion

以上的较大数字的区间。汉语中的"万"只能译作 ten thousand,"十万"译作 a hundred thousand,"千万"译作 ten million,"亿"则译成 a hundred million。这种不同的区间划分给汉英数字互译带来了很大麻烦,因为翻译时译员必须进行单位区间的转换。

8.2.2 大数字口译方法

在口译过程中遇到大数字时,译员必须借助笔记来完成翻译。由于英汉数字单位不同,口译大数字时需要进行单位区间的转换,而只有通过强化培训,译员才能熟练掌握大数字间的英汉互译,避免发生错误。以下介绍三种常见的训练方法。

1. 模板式训练

首先,将汉英对应的数字单位标在表格里(如表 8–5 所示);其次,在进行大数字口译时,把相应的数字填在表格里;最后,经过这种反复的训练,达到即使没有表格存在,译员也能即时进行数字间的转换。

表 8–5　中英大数字模板式训练表

兆	千亿	百亿	十亿	亿	千万	百万	十万	万	千	百	十	个
trillion			billion			million			thousand			

2. 运用上下标"'"","进行数字分割

将听到的整数先用阿拉伯数字记录下来,再运用上下标"'"","进行数字分割,如用"'"表示汉语数字"0000"万位,用","表示英语数字"000"千位,最后用目标语读出。若是英译汉数字,就在数字上方从后向前每四位用上标"'"进行标记;若是汉译英数字,就在数字下方从后向前每三位用下标","进行标记。例如:

第八章　数字口译

- 500 thousand = 50' = 50 万
- 5 million = 500' = 5 百万
- 5 千 = 5, = 5 thousand
- 5 万 = 50, = 50 thousand

3. 小数点移位法

在汉译英时，可以用小数点移位法，把汉语大数字转换成英语的数字单位 th、m、b、tri。例如：

- 965 万 = 9.65 m
- 578.3 亿 = 57.83 b
- 15 000 亿 = 1.5 tri

> 技巧训练：听下列录音，进行口译数字练习。

练习六　英译汉（1—20）

练习七　汉译英（1—20）

> 技巧训练：口译下列句子。

练习八　视译

1) With an area of 7,692,024 square kilometers, Australia is one of the largest countries on Earth and the only country that covers an entire continent.

2) The population of Australia is estimated to be 25,722,500 as of December 30, 2020, according to the latest United Nations data.

3）The gross domestic product in Australia was worth $1,392.70 billion in 2019, according to the official data from the World Bank and projections from *Trading Economics*, representing 1.16% of the world economy.

4）In 2019, approximately 9.4 million tourists visited Australia from overseas.

5）China is Australia's biggest trading partner for both the export and import of goods. The value of goods exported from Australia to China doubled in the five years from $75 billion in 2014-2015 to $150 billion in 2019-2020.

6）Australia has enjoyed a decade-long boom in international education. International student revenue at all Australian universities hit 8.9 billion Australian dollars in 2018.

7）Australia is home to an estimated 570,000 different species, giving it more than 5% of the world's plants and animals.

8）Sydney is Australia's largest city with about 5 million inhabitants, which means that about 20% of all Australians live in this metropolitan city.

9）中国占地面积约 960 万平方公里，陆地边界长达 2 万多公里。从东到西相距 5 200 多公里，从北到南相距 5 500 多公里。

10）中国的海岸线长约 1.8 万公里，海域面积为 473 万平方公里，包括渤海、黄海、东海和南海，以及台湾以东的太平洋海域。

11）北京是中华人民共和国的首都，占地面积约 1.78 万平方公里，人口有 1 000 万。北京建于公元 937 年，作为首都已有 800 多年的历史。

12）中国数字经济蓬勃发展，移动支付用户已经超过 5 亿，正引领全球支付体系迈入新时代。

13）中国货物进出口总额超过 30 万亿元，实际使用外资 1 383 亿美元，稳居发展中国家首位。

14）2018 年《福布斯》中国慈善榜上榜的 100 位企业家现金捐赠总额为 173.1 亿元，同比上涨 66%。

15）仅 2017 年的"腾讯 99 公益日"就吸引 1 000 多万人参与，捐赠量突破 13 亿元。

16）中国目前已同138个国家和30个国际组织签署200份共建"一带一路"合作文件，累计向沿线国家投资超过1 000亿美元，为东道国创造税收超过40亿美元、就业岗位近37万个。

练习九　听译（1—16）

8.3 经贸合作口译

8.3.1 经贸合作译前准备

A. 词汇

- 多边贸易体制：multilateral trade system
- 社会主义市场经济体制：socialist market economy system
- 保护主义：protectionism
- 单边主义：unilateralism
- 经济霸权主义：economic hegemony
- 相互尊重：mutual respect
- 平等协商：equal consultation
- 互利共赢：mutually beneficial and win-win outcomes
- 进口关税：tariff
- 约束关税：bound tariff
- 关税配额管理：tariff rate quota administration
- 中小微企业：micro, small, and medium-sized enterprises
- 民营企业：private companies
- 外商投资企业：foreign-invested enterprises
- 外商独资企业：foreign-owned enterprises

- 外商直接投资: foreign direct investment (FDI)
- 投资便利化: investment facilitation
- 外贸经营权备案登记制: registration system for foreign trade authorization
- 反倾销措施: anti-dumping measures against...
- 风险管理/评估: risk management/assessment
- 国际清算: international settlement
- 国际收支平衡: balance of international payments / balance of payments
- 国际收支不平衡: disequilibrium in the balance of international payments
- 国家补贴: public subsidies
- 国家鼓励项目: projects listed as encouraged by the state
- 季节性调价: seasonal price adjustments
- 坏帐、呆帐、死帐: bad account / dead account / non-collectable account / bad debt / bad loan
- 减免债务: reduce and cancel debts
- 经常性的财政收入: regular revenues
- 超前消费: deficit spending
- 企业亏损补贴: subsidies to cover enterprise losses
- 电子商务: e-commerce
- 自由贸易: free trade
- 无纸交易: paperless transaction
- 争端解决机制: dispute settlement mechanism
- 政府采购: government procurement
- 贸易顺/逆差: trade surplus/deficit
- 贸易纠纷: trade disputes
- 询价: inquiry
- 报价: offer

第八章 数字口译

- 实盘：firm offer
- 成本加运费价：cost and freight (C&F)
- 成本、保险加运费价（到岸价）：cost, insurance and freight (CIF)
- 离岸价：free on board (FOB)
- 付款交单：documents against payment (D/P)
- 承兑交单：documents against acceptance (D/A)
- 一般原产地证：certificate of origin (CO)
- 普惠制：generalized system of preferences (GSP)
- 销售确认书：sales contract (SC)
- 信用证：letter of credit (LC)
- 电汇：telegraphic transfer (TT)
- 提单：bill of lading (BL)
- 大幅度降低进口关税：substantively reduce import tariffs
- 显著削减非关税壁垒：significantly lower non-tariff barriers
- 全面放开外贸经营权：fully liberalize the right to foreign trade
- 提高市场意识、竞争意识、规则意识以及法制观念：raise public awareness of the market, competition, rules, and concept of rule of law
- 完善法治化、国际化、便利化的营商环境：cultivate a business environment that is law-based, internationalized, and business-friendly
- "一带一路"国际合作高峰论坛：Belt and Road Forum for International Cooperation
- 博鳌亚洲论坛：Boao Forum for Asia
- 世界经济论坛：World Economic Forum
- 金砖国家峰会：BRICS Summit
- 亚太经合组织领导人非正式会议：APEC Economic Leaders' Meeting
- 二十国集团领导人峰会：G20 Summit

- 国家知识产权局: National Intellectual Property Administration
- 中华人民共和国商务部: Ministry of Commerce, PRC

B. 背景知识

- 世界贸易组织: World Trade Organization (WTO)

The World Trade Organization is the only global international organization dealing with the rules of trade between nations. At its heart are the WTO agreements, negotiated and signed by the bulk of the world's trading nations and ratified in their parliaments. The goal is to ensure that trade flows as smoothly, predictably, and freely as possible. The WTO has over 160 members representing 98% of world trade. To join the WTO, a government has to bring its economic and trade policies in line with WTO rules and negotiate its terms of entry with the WTO membership.

The WTO has many roles: It operates a global system of trade rules, it acts as a forum for negotiating trade agreements, it settles trade disputes between its members, and it supports the needs of developing countries. All major decisions are made by the WTO member governments: either by ministers (who usually meet at least every two years) or by their ambassadors or delegates (who meet regularly in Geneva). The current Director-General is Ngozi Okonjo-Iweala.

- 知识产权: intellectual property (IP)

It is a category of property that includes intangible creations of the human intellect. There are many types of intellectual property, and the most well-known types are copyrights, patents, trademarks, and trade secrets.

The main purpose of intellectual property law is to encourage the creation of a wide variety of intellectual goods. To achieve this, the law gives people and businesses property rights to the information and intellectual goods they create, usually for a limited period of time. This gives economic incentive for their creation, because it allows people to profit from the information and intellectual goods they create.

- 经济全球化: economic globalization

Economic globalization refers to the widespread international movement of goods, capital, services, technology, and information. It is the increasing economic integration and interdependence of national, regional, and local economies across the world through an intensification of cross-border movement of goods, services, technology, and capital. Economic globalization primarily comprises the globalization of production, finance, markets, technology, organizational regimes, institutions, corporations, and labor.

The fast globalization of the world's economies in recent years is largely based on the rapid development of science and technology, has resulted from the environment in which market economic system has been fast spreading throughout the world, and has developed on the basis of increasing cross-border division of labor that has been penetrating down to the level of production chains within enterprises of different countries.

- 中国"十四五"时期经济社会发展主要目标: China's priority goals for social and economic development during the 14th Five-Year Plan period (2021–2025)

The goals are new progress in economic development, further reform and opening-up, greater civility in the public sphere, notable progress in eco-civilization, improvement in the people's well-being, and more effective state governance.

- "两个一百年"奋斗目标: Two Centenary Goals

The Two Centenary Goals were put forth by the CPC at its 18th National

Congress in November 2012 for building socialism with Chinese characteristics. The two goals are to complete a moderately prosperous society in all respects by the centenary of the CPC and to build China into a modern socialist country that is prosperous, strong, democratic, culturally advanced, and harmonious by the centenary of the PRC.

8.3.2 经贸合作连续口译

> 课堂练习：口译下列语段，注意英汉数字之间的转换。

练习十　视译

1) In 2017, our bilateral trade volume hit a record high of 26.1 billion New Zealand dollars, making China become New Zealand's largest partner in the trade of goods. Two ways of investments reached more than 10 billion New Zealand dollars in accumulative manner. People-to-people exchanges also flourished. There were more than 400,000 Chinese visitors to New Zealand last year. As a result, more airlines operate between China and New Zealand, with 80 direct flights every week in peak seasons.

2) Free and open trade spurs innovation, rewards enterprise, and fosters mutual security. It allows people to improve their own lives. The exchange of goods and services gives them access to global opportunities, sharing knowledge, skills, and experience. Trade liberalization, globalization, and integration have gone hand in hand with a boom era of international trade. Since joining the WTO in 2001, China has become the world's largest exporter, and in turn, it has brought more than 1.4 billion consumers into the global market place.

3) 我昨天碰巧看到几个有意思的数字，愿同大家分享。中国一天有8万多辆汽车销售一空，8 000多万个快递包裹流动传递，全国各地放映

第八章　数字口译

22万场电影，4 200列高速列车奔驰在中国大地上，40多万吨粮食被消费。这仅仅是关于中国一天的数字，大家不难发现其中蕴含的巨大商机。中国这样一个大市场，必将是世界经济增长的动力所在、稳定所在、活力所在！

4）以世贸组织为核心的多边贸易体制是国际贸易的基石，是全球贸易健康有序发展的支柱。中国自2001年加入世贸组织以来，坚决遵守和维护世贸组织规则，支持开放、透明、包容、非歧视的多边贸易体制，全面参与世贸组织工作，为共同完善全球经济治理发出中国声音、提出中国方案，是多边贸易体制的积极参与者、坚定维护者和重要贡献者。

练习十一　听译（1—4）

课堂练习：听下列录音，进行连续口译。

练习十二　Celebrating Trading Opportunities Between China and the U.K.

背景知识

Baroness Fairhead: 费厚德女男爵。Baroness Fairhead serves for the Minister of State for Trade and Export Promotion, the Department for International Trade.

Canary Wharf: 伦敦金丝雀码头。It is a commercial estate on the Isle of Dogs in London, in the London Borough of Tower Hamlets. As one of the main financial centers of the United Kingdom, along with the City of London, it contains around 16 million square feet (1.5 million square meters) of office and retail space. Around 105,000 people work there. It is home to the world or European headquarters of numerous major banks, professional services firms, and media organizations. There are over 300 shops, cafes, bars, and restaurants, a cinema, one of London's biggest roof gardens, and one of the U.K.'s largest, free to visit, collections of public art. It offers a fantastic program of music, film, theater, dance, art, fashion, and more throughout the year.

Wolverhampton Wanderers：伍尔弗汉普顿流浪足球俱乐部。It is commonly known as Wolves, a professional football club in Wolverhampton, West Midlands, England. Formed as St. Luke's F. C. in 1877, it has played at Molineux Stadium since 1889 and currently competes in the Premier League, the top tier of English football. The club is now owned by Fosun International Limited (复星国际), a Chinese international conglomerate and investment company.

Aston Villa Football Club：阿斯顿维拉足球俱乐部。It is a professional football club based in Aston, Birmingham, England. Founded in 1874, it has played at its current home ground, Villa Park, since 1897. Aston Villa is one of the founder members of the Football League in 1888 and of the Premier League in 1992. It is one of only five English clubs to have won the European Cup, in 1981–1982. It has also won the Football League First Division seven times, the FA Cup seven times, the League Cup five times, and the UEFA Super Cup once. Aston Villa was taken over by Recon Group (睿康集团) headquartered in Beijing in 2016.

Offshore wind in Scotland：苏格兰离岸风力发电站。The U.K. government is keen to engage with Chinese offshore wind opportunities. The British innovation agent Innovate U.K. funded the launch of a new platform to support U.K. companies providing technical solutions to wind farm issues for Chinese partners. There are a series of Chinese investments in the United Kingdom's offshore wind sector. In 2015, China Three Gorges Corporation (三峡集团) bought a 30% stake in the Scotland-based Moray

Firth offshore project, from Portuguese developer EDP Renováveis. In 2016, China's state-owned investment holding company State Development and Investment Corporation (国家开发投资集团) acquired the U.K. wind power activities of Spanish energy company Repsol, for €238 million ($282 million). And in 2017, state-owned conglomerate China Resources National Corporation (华润集团) bought a 30% stake in a British offshore wind farm for £600 million ($803 million).

练习十三 中国驻新西兰大使吴玺在"三城经济联盟"峰会活动上的致辞

 背景知识

三城经济联盟：The Tripartite Economic Alliance was signed in 2014 in Guangzhou, and aims to help create jobs and enhance trade, investment, and economic opportunities between sister cities Auckland, Los Angeles, and Guangzhou.

第九章 习语口译

　　习语是语言的精髓，承载着浓厚的民族色彩和丰富的文化内涵。习语一般是指具有特定形式的词组，其蕴含的意义不是从词组中单个词的意思推测而来的，而是必须作为一个整体来理解。习语中词的结构、顺序和使用都是固定的，不能随意更改或替换。从广义上讲，习语包含了某种语言中所有的惯用语和特殊表达，如英语习语包括俗语、谚语和俚语等，汉语习语包括成语、俗语、谚语和歇后语等。

　　英汉两种语言都拥有大量的习语，它们与各自独特的历史、地理、风俗、生活、价值观、宗教信仰等有着不可分割的联系，反映出各自民族的文化特色，因此存在较大的差异。在口译时，译员必须了解英汉习语的文化和历史背景，并能够使用各种技巧来进行翻译。习语的口译策略可以大致归纳为以下四种。

9.1 习语对译法

　　英汉两种语言都富含习语，有些英语习语和汉语习语尽管表现手法不同，但无论在意义、形象或风格上都比较相似或相近。那么在这种情况下可以使用等值借用法，即以习语译习语（idiom for idiom）。例如：

英译汉

- The same knife cuts bread and fingers.

  水能载舟，亦能覆舟。

- A new broom sweeps clean.

  新官上任三把火

- A young idler, an old beggar.

  少壮不努力，老大徒伤悲。

- Walls have ears.

  隔墙有耳

- gild the lily

  画蛇添足

汉译英

- 英雄所见略同

  Great minds think alike.

- 冰冻三尺非一日之寒

  Rome is not built in a day.

- 有志者事竟成

  Where there is a will, there is a way.

- 种瓜得瓜，种豆得豆。

  As you sow, so will you reap.

- 佛要金装，人要衣装。

  Fine feathers make fine birds.

9.2 直译法

直译（literal translation）是指完全保留源语习语的意义，使内容与形式相符的方法。许多习语有着生动、形象的比喻，为了让这些比喻能够被听者很容易地理解和接受，在不违背文化传统的前提下可以使用直译法。这不仅能保持原文的意义，还能保持原文的形式。例如：

英译汉

- A stitch in time saves nine.

  一针及时顶九针

- Seeing is believing.

  眼见为实

- as light as a feather

  轻如鸿毛

- arm to the teeth

  武装到牙齿

- show one's cards

  摊牌

汉译英

- 君子动口不动手

  A gentleman uses his tongue, not his fists.

- 眼不见，心不烦。

  Out of sight, out of mind.

- 打破纪录

  break the record

- 血浓于水

  Blood is thicker than water.

- 己所不欲，勿施于人。

  Don't do to others what you don't want others to do to you.

9.3 意译法

有些习语具有浓厚的民族和地方文化特色，在翻译时既不能借用译入语的习语来表达，又不能使用直译法来翻译，因为这样会引起误解或者不被译入语使用者接受。在这种情况下需要舍弃原文的字面意义，并将其隐含的意义表达出来，从而使译文与原文的内容相符及主要语言功能相似，这种方法就是意译法（paraphrasing）。例如：

英译汉

- let the cat out of the bag

    泄露秘密

- a fat cat

    大款

- like a fish out of water

    很不自在

- born with a silver spoon in one's mouth

    生在富贵之家

- rain cats and dogs

    瓢泼大雨

汉译英

- 忠言逆耳利于行

    Unpleasant advice is a good medicine.

- 新手

    a green hand

- 望子成龙

    expect one's son to be somebody

- 萝卜白菜，各有所爱。

People have different tastes.

- 司马昭之心，路人皆知。

The ill intention is all too clear for anyone to see.

9.4 直译加注法

对于一些习语，特别是涉及历史典故、文学名著的习语，若用直译法，译文难以理解；若用意译法，译文会失去原文具有的风格；直译加注法（literal translation combined with paraphrasing）不仅能够保持原文具有的意义、形象与风格，体现出某种语言特有的文化特色，还可以将其深刻内涵一并展现出来。例如：

英译汉

- meet one's Waterloo

  遭遇滑铁卢（一败涂地）

- an apple of discord

  纠纷的苹果（争斗之源、祸根）

- Procrustean bed

  普洛克路斯忒斯之床（削足适履、强求一致）

- a pound of flesh

  要求偿还一磅肉（合法但极不合理的事）

- the Trojan horse

  特洛伊木马／木马计（暗藏的危险、奸细）

汉译英

- 刘姥姥进了大观园

  Granny Liu entered the great palace—a countryman's awe with the splendid environment.

- 三个臭皮匠，赛过诸葛亮。

  Three cobblers with their wits combined surpass Zhuge Liang the mastermind—two heads are better than one.

- 杀鸡儆猴

  to kill the chicken to frighten the monkey—to punish somebody as a warning to others

- 班门弄斧

  to show off one's skill with the axe before Lu Ban the master carpenter—to display one's skill before an expert

- 阿 Q 精神

  the spirit of Ah Q—spiritual victory (Ah Q, the main character in Lu Xun's *The True Story of Ah Q*, a backward peasant who interprets his defeats as moral victories)

技巧训练：口译下列习语。

练习一　视译

1) go bananas

2) hard cheese

3) Every dog has its day.

4) lucky dog

5) to know the ropes

6) to burn one's boat

7) black sheep

8) at sixes and sevens

9) like father like son

10) at the eleventh hour

第九章 习语口译

11）错失良机

12）一贫如洗

13）一箭双雕

14）削足适履

15）一个和尚挑水吃，两个和尚抬水吃，三个和尚没水吃。

16）金无足赤，人无完人。

17）路遥知马力，日久见人心。

18）小巫见大巫

19）滴水穿石

20）阿谀奉承

练习二　听译（1—20）

技巧训练：口译下列带有习语的句子。

练习三　视译

1）Let's not beat about the bush—they rejected it.

2）None of that delegate's arguments seems to hold water.

3）You can't have your cake and eat it.

4）The proof of the pudding is in the eating.

5）If you support your son, your business partner will be hurt, and vice versa. You're caught between the devil and the deep blue sea.

6）He plays piano like nobody's business.

7）When Michael was born, I was on cloud nine. I couldn't believe this beautiful little boy was ours.

8) He was fed up with people bending his ear about staying on at school or what he should do afterwards. He wanted to think it out himself.

9) Mr. Clarke had a face like thunder after his assistant made a mistake.

10) Clients should know better than to take the advice of a wholesaler at face value.

11) 我衷心希望，参会参展的各国朋友都能广结良缘、满载而归！

12) 在这个进程中，各国经济不同程度地融入其中，彼此相互依存、共生共荣。

13) 哈佛大学是世界著名的高等学府，精英荟萃，人才辈出。

14) 如果你们到中国东南沿海城市旅行，就会看到高楼林立、车流如织、灯火辉煌的现代景观。

15) 我们都已深切地感受到贵国在改革开放政策的引导下，气象万千，充满活力，不断进步。

16) 大国之间不仅可以和而不同、求同存异，而且能够聚同化异、优势互补。

17) 火中取栗最终只会引火烧身。

18) 中英都是拥有悠久历史和灿烂文化的伟大国家，两国人民都是执着追求、自强不息的伟大人民。

19) 冰冻三尺非一日之寒。尽管隧道的尽头已经显露曙光，但前行的道路不可能一帆风顺。

20) 文明永续发展，既需要薪火相传、代代守护，更需要顺时应势、推陈出新。

练习四　听译（1—20）

第九章 习语口译

9.5 人文交流口译

9.5.1 人文交流译前准备

A. 词汇

- 人文交流：people-to-people and cultural exchanges
- 交流互鉴：exchanges and mutual learning
- 和睦相处：live in harmony
- 互尊互信：respect and trust each other
- 文化遗产：cultural heritage
- 文化设施：cultural facilities
- 四大发明：the four great inventions of ancient China
- 火药：gunpowder
- 印刷术：printing / art of printing
- 造纸术：papermaking technology
- 指南针：compass
- 中国书法：Chinese calligraphy
- 中国结：Chinese knot
- 剪纸：paper cuttings
- 刺绣：embroidery
- 中国画：Chinese painting
- 太极：Tai Chi
- 武术：Chinese martial arts / Kung Fu
- 京剧：Peking Opera
- 杂技：acrobatics
- 社会习俗：rituals / social customs

- 民间传说: folk tales
- 底格里斯河: the Tigris
- 幼发拉底河: the Euphrates
- 印度河: the Indus
- 恒河: the Ganges
- 《红楼梦》: *A Dream in Red Mansions / The Story of the Stone*
- 《聊斋志异》: *Strange Tales of a Lonely Studio*
- 《论语》: *Analects of Confucius*
- 《三国演义》: *The Romance of the Three Kingdoms*
- 《山海经》: *The Classic of Mountains and Rivers*
- 《西游记》: *Pilgrimage to the West / Journey to the West*
- 《资治通鉴》: *History as a Mirror*
- 《水浒传》: *Heroes of the Marshes / Water Margins*
- 中华人民共和国文化和旅游部: Ministry of Culture and Tourism, PRC
- 国家文物局: State Administration of Cultural Relics

B. 背景知识

- 命运共同体: a community of shared future

The idea of building a community of shared future was first discussed in a report to the 18th CPC National Congress in 2012. It was seen as contributing to China's engagement with the rest of the world in pursuit of win-win results. The idea has since become a core element of China's foreign policy.

The concept of a community of shared future emphasizes the virtue of holistic thinking, cosmopolitan ideals, and the pursuit of lasting peace and shared prosperity. The destiny of a country should be in the hands of its people, and the future of the world must be shaped jointly by the peoples of the world. A country's national interests are to be pursued with other countries' interests in mind. The implementation of any national development strategy should be accompanied by careful consideration of the development needs of other countries.

- 文化全球化: cultural globalization

Cultural globalization refers to the transmission of ideas, meanings, and values around the world in such a way as to extend and intensify social relations. This process is marked by the common consumption of cultures that have been diffused by the Internet, popular culture media, and international travel. This has added to processes of commodity exchange and colonization which have a longer history of carrying cultural meaning around the globe. The circulation of cultures enables individuals to partake in extended social relations that cross national and regional borders. The creation and expansion of such social relations are not merely observed on a material level. Cultural globalization involves the formation of shared norms and knowledge with which people associate their individual and collective cultural identities.

- 文化外交: cultural diplomacy

Cultural diplomacy is a type of public diplomacy and soft power that includes the exchange of ideas, information, art, language, and other aspects of culture among nations and their peoples in order to foster mutual understanding. Ultimately, the goal of cultural diplomacy is to influence a foreign audience and use that influence, which is built up over the long term, as a sort of goodwill reserve to win support for policies. It seeks to harness the elements of culture to induce foreigners to have a positive view of the country's people, culture, and policies, to induce greater cooperation between the two nations, to aid in changing the policies or political environment of the target nation, and to prevent, manage, and mitigate conflicts with the target nation. In turn, cultural diplomacy can help a nation better understand the foreign nation it is engaged with and it fosters mutual understanding.

- 中华传统文化理念：Chinese traditional cultural concept

China is a multinational country with a long history and splendid culture. In China, people believe in "seeking happiness in good deeds". In the words of the sages, "He is a man of virtue who offers financial help to many," and "To establish oneself, one should help others establish themselves." For Chinese civilization, amity and good neighborliness is the principle guiding its interactions with other countries; to deliver prosperity and security to the people is the overarching goal, to keep pace with the times through reform and innovation is the abiding commitment, and to achieve harmony between man and nature is the underlying philosophy.

- 中国新发展理念：China's new concept of development

The new concept of pursuing innovative, coordinated, green and open development and having its fruits shared by everyone was listed in a report to the 19th CPC National Congress as one of the 14 points of China's basic policy for the new era. Innovation is the driving force for development; coordination involves sustainable and healthy development; green is the guarantee for sustainable development; open reinforces China's commitment to international cooperation; and to be shared means that the development fruits are shared by all. This is the basic principle of socialism.

9.5.2 人文交流连续口译

课堂练习：口译下列语段，注意习语翻译技巧的应用。

第九章 习语口译

练习五 视译

1) All over the world, we have different cultures, traditions, and lifestyles, but if we look closely, we will find that there are many things that connect us together, and there are too many things that we have in common, but in different external forms. When reading Chinese stories, I was reminded at times of *Aesop's Fables*—tales that contain simple, moral messages that appeal to our shared humanity, yet which are uniquely coded to the varying ethical leanings of different peoples. Likewise, at times I found myself thinking of Shakespeare, particularly during the instances of murder, suicide, and betrayal. I was at once fascinated by the historical and philosophical insights into ancient China that the stories offered.

2) Asia is home to one of the earliest human settlements and an important cradle of human civilizations. This vast and beautiful continent covers a third of the Earth's land mass and has two thirds of the world's population. It has more than 1,000 ethnic groups living in 47 countries. For several thousand years before the Common Era, our forefathers living along the Tigris and the Euphrates, the Indus and the Ganges, the Yellow River and the Yangtze, tilled and irrigated the land, made tools and utensils, and built homes to live in. Generation after generation, our ancestors in Asia, with their tireless endeavors, created a time-honored history and a profound and rich civilization.

3) 自古以来，中华文明在继承创新中不断发展，在应时处变中不断升华，积淀着中华民族最深沉的精神追求，是中华民族生生不息、发展壮大的丰厚滋养。中国的造纸术、火药、印刷术、指南针、天文历法、哲学思想、民本理念等在世界上影响深远，有力推动了人类文明发展进程。

4) 深化人文交流互鉴是消除隔阂和误解、促进民心相知相通的重要途径。这些年来，中国同各国一道，在教育、文化、体育、卫生等领域搭建了众多合作平台，开辟了广泛合作渠道。中国愿同各国加强青少年、民间团体、地方组织、媒体等各界交流，打造智库交流合作网络，创新合作模式，推动各种形式的合作走深走实，为推动文明交流互鉴创造条件。

练习六　听译（1—4）

> 课堂练习：听下列录音，进行连续口译。

练习七　Speech for the Commemoration of 40 Years of China's Reform and Opening-up

背景知识

2018年12月11日上午，中国驻英国大使馆在伦敦西敏市中央礼堂隆重举行中国改革开放40周年主题纪念活动。"全球化"概念的首创者之一马丁·阿尔布劳在致辞中表示，不是西方的全球化推动了中国的改革开放，而是中国的改革开放开启了世界全球化的进程。中国对外开放比西方全球化拥有更全面的视角，体现了国与国之间的互利互惠以及不同文化之间的和谐共赢。习近平主席提出的"一带一路"倡议和构建人类命运共同体的理念，是中国对全球治理体系改革的重大贡献。

The Freedom of the City of London: 伦敦金融城"荣誉市民"。这是伦敦金融城授予的最高荣誉，以表彰在相关领域做出突出贡献的人士。2018年12月3日，伦敦金融城授予中国驻英国大使刘晓明"荣誉市民"称号。

第九章 习语口译

练习八 中国驻英国大使馆马辉公使在马恩岛华人协会5周年庆典上的讲话

背景知识

The Isle of Man: 马恩岛。It is a self-governing British Crown dependency. The head of state is Queen Elizabeth Ⅱ who holds the title of Lord of Man and is represented by a lieutenant governor. The United Kingdom is responsible for the island's defense, ultimately for good governance, and for representing the island in international forums, while the island's own parliament and government have competence over all domestic matters. It is located in the middle of the northern Irish Sea, almost equidistant from England, Northern Ireland, Scotland (closest), and Wales (farthest). It is 52 kilometers (32 miles) long and, at its widest point, 22 kilometers (14 miles) wide. It has an area of around 572 square kilometers (221 square miles). Douglas is its capital. The culture of the Isle of Man is often promoted as being influenced by its Celtic. The official language of the Isle of Man is English. Manx has traditionally been spoken but is now considered "critically endangered".

Isle of Man Chinese Association: 马恩岛华人协会。该协会成立于2013年9月，是马恩岛华人发起的非营利组织，致力于弘扬中华文化，推动中国与马恩岛以及中英两国之间的友好交往与合作。

第十章 口译的应变策略

口译是一种特殊的跨语言、跨文化交际行为。由于口译的即时性、现场性和限时性，无论是新手还是资深译员，他们都会在口译过程中遇到各种各样的突发状况。为了保证口译工作的顺利进行，译员需要具备一定的临场应变能力，掌握一定的应变策略，以便克服口译过程中出现的各种障碍，出色地完成口译任务。

10.1 译员的应变能力

译员的应变能力是指在口译过程中出现突发状况时，译员使用策略的能力。鉴于口译现场的复杂性，译员需要反应灵活、思维敏捷，在不影响传达源语主要信息和说话者主要意图的基础上，适当采用应变策略，及时处理口译过程中出现的问题，以保证交际渠道的畅通。这种临场发挥、随机应变的能力是译员口译能力的体现。

10.2 口译的应变策略

口译的应变策略是指在口译过程中出现突发状况时，译员应该在何种情况下采用何种策略解决口译问题，从而使交际顺利地进行。口译的应变策略包括以下五个方面：词的处理、数字的处理、概括与省略、语言功能对等和禁忌话题处理。

10.2.1 词的处理

1. 上下文猜词

在口译过程中，当译员漏听某个词语或遇到生词时，一是可以通过前后话语的同义词、反义词、举例、重复、解释等猜出词义。例如，"Hong Kong is constantly changing, and it can never get stagnant."，如果不知道 stagnant 的意思，译员可以通过前文的 constantly changing 和 never 知道这个词是 constantly changing 的反义词，进而得出整句话的意思为"香港不断变化，永远不会停滞不前"。又如，"The implication is that they should be left alone: no paternalistic government telling people what to do, believing that it knows what is good for them."，如果不知道 paternalistic government 是什么样的"政府"，译员可以通过后边的分词词组 telling people what to do 和宾语从句 believing that it knows what is good for them 猜出是"家长式作风"，所以整句话可以译为"言外之意是政府不应该管他们，不应该有家长式作风，告诉他们该做什么，认为它知道什么对他们好"。再如，"The new tax law supersedes, or replaces, the law that was in effect last year."，如果 supersede 是生词，译员可以根据其后边紧接着用 or 引出的同义词 replace 的词义，推断出 supersede 的大概意思是"取代""接替"，所以整句话可以译为"新税法取代了去年执行的法律"。

二是根据已有的背景知识推断词义。如果译员对口译内容和背景有足够的了解，那么即使漏听某个词或遇到某些生词，也不会影响他对整句话的理解。例如，"If you've ever had surgery, unless you are super tough, you've gone through it with the benefit of anesthetics."，根据医学常识，病人做手术前需要麻醉，译员可以很容易地推断出 anesthetics 是"麻醉剂"的意思，所以整句话可以译为"如果你曾经做过手术，除非你超级坚强，否则你的手术是在麻醉下进行的"。如果猜不出词义，而这个词的意思又非常关键，译员可以通过询问讲话人或现场的专家，把意思补充完整。当然，这种策略是不得已而为之的，使用次数不宜过多，否则听众会质疑译员的口译能力，对译员失去信心。

2. 释义

释义是口译中一种重要的语言重组技巧，是为了避免因找不到对应词出现卡壳或中断口译而采取的一种策略。当译员不知道或者突然忘记某个词的含义时，他可以使用同属一个集合里的更具概括性的词语来指代该词，或用上义词来取代下义词。上义词针对的是共性，是对事物的概括性、抽象性说明，而下义词针对的是个性，是对事物的具体表现形式或更为具体的说明。例如，若译员不知道"红冠亚马孙鹦鹉"的英语对应词是 Amazona viridigenalis，他可以用词组 a red-crowned parrot（带有红色冠子的鹦鹉）进行替代翻译，又不妨把该词的信息内涵扩大，用更具概括性的词组 a kind of parrot（某种鹦鹉），或鹦鹉的上义词 a kind of bird（某类鸟）来表述，这都不失为一个好办法。

当某一词语在译入语中找不到对应的词语时，如新词语，译员也可以通过释义的办法来解决。所谓新词语是指内涵新、形式新，原来的词汇系统中没有的或虽有但内涵是全新的词语。这些词语都是特定社会发展、变化的产物，有其特殊的时代背景，但无法在译入语中找到完全能把其内涵和字面意思生动形象地结合起来的对应词语。在数字时代，随着人工智能的发展，出现了很多与数字、网络相关的新词语，如汉语里的"锦鲤"（泛指在小概率事件中运气极佳的人）、"官宣"（从"官网""官微"衍生而来，意为"官方宣布"。"官方"本指政府方面，如"官方人士""官方消息"等，而把个人、机构等非官方行为称为"官方"，有强调其权威性、可靠性的意思）、"退群"（指退出某个社交平台上的交流小组。后来，随着含义的引申和使用范围的扩大，退群也指退出某一群体），等等；英语里的动词 instagram（Instagram 原本是一款图片共享应用程序，这里指用一种快速、美妙和有趣的方式将随时抓拍的图片发布到 Instagram 上进行照片共享）、名词 fintech（意思是金融科技，即用新开发的数字和网络技术提高金融体系效率的产品或公司）、force quit（指因点击频繁，电脑无响应而强行关机），等等。

又如，近两年，国内外社交网络上出现的常用词语 bots（"机器人"，即由算法操作的自动的社交媒体账号）、botnets（"水军"，即由相同的个人或者组织管理的机器人账号的网络，主要出现在推特和其他允许用户创建多个账户的社交网络上）和 trolls（"喷子"，即在社交网络上故意发表挑衅或者跑题帖子来挑起网络冲突或者冒犯他人，从而转移注意力、制造分裂的人）。在英汉互译时，合理的释义有助于双方达到理解与交流的目的。

3. 音译

当遇到无法在译入语中找到对应词的专业术语时，译员可以通过重复源语的发音进行音译。由于同一领域内的专家使用的专业术语基本上是相通的，音译可以使双方达到相互理解和沟通的目的，使交流顺畅地进行下去。例如，当谈及有关网络的 Twitter、Google、Wi-Fi 时，可以直接音译为 ['twɪtə(r)]、['guːgl]、['waɪˌfaɪ]。比如 Wi-Fi，不必翻译成"无线局域网"，因为大多数人都知道它是什么意思，更何况是业界人士。音译法还可以适用于人名、地名、组织名称等的翻译。

10.2.2 数字的处理

1. 模糊数字代替具体数字

当遇到没有听清具体内容的大数字时，或遇到数字密集、列举信息繁多等情况时，译员可以采用模糊处理的方式，用模糊整数代替具体数字。例如，"In 2017, China topped the world both in the number of people traveling abroad, which was 143 million, and in tourist expenditure overseas, which was 257.7 billion dollars."，译员可以把大数字处理译为"2017年中国出境旅游人数达 1.4 亿多人次，出境旅游支出额达近 2 580 亿美元，均位居世界第一"。

2. 非等值对应

在口译数字时，汉英互译有可能出现数字不对等的情况，这时就需要译员灵活处理，使译入语更符合汉语或英语的表达方式，从而沟通可以顺利进行。例如：

汉译英

- 一朝被蛇咬，十年怕井绳。

  Once bitten, twice shy.

- 这方面，我认为干一寸胜过说一尺。

  In this regard, even a small action is a lot more important than a thousand words.

- 九死一生

  a narrow escape from death

- 五十步笑百步

  The pot calls the kettle black.

- 接二连三

  one after another

英译汉

- Seven hours' sleep will make a clown forget his design.

  贪睡会让小丑忘记自己的看家本领。

- Keep a thing seven years and you will find a use for it.

  东西放着总会有用。

- I'll love you three scores and ten.

  我会一辈子爱你的。

- I always believe my sixth sense.

  我总是相信我的直觉。

- Ten to one he has forgotten it.

他十有八九已经忘了。

10.2.3 概括与省略

东西方在文化传统、思维方式、审美习惯等方面有很大的不同，表现在语言方面是汉语的遣词造句辞藻华丽，善用叠词，特别讲求工整对仗，追求意美、音美和形美；英语重写实、重逻辑，句式严谨，表达缜密，用词简洁。所以，在汉译英时，在保持源语主旨不变的前提下，需要概括或省略部分冗余信息，使译文注重客观，更凝练、紧凑、明了。例如，汉语"胜利召开""刻苦勤奋""毫无根据的诽谤""不切实际的幻想""多才多艺""年终岁末"中的修饰词符合汉语的行文习惯，意义重复却不显得累赘。但是，这类修饰词若直译为英语，就会显得意思重复、不合逻辑。在汉译英时需要对这类词的意义及用途仔细斟酌，必要时进行概括或省略。例如，"中国将尊重国际营商惯例，对在中国境内注册的各类企业一视同仁、平等对待"，显然，"一视同仁"和"平等对待"的含义相同，在口译时可概括译为："We respect international business rules and practices, and provide equal treatment to all types of businesses registered in China."。

在口译过程中，遇到讲话人语速过快、信息密集堆砌、图表繁多等情况时，译员只能采取概括与省略部分信息的办法。例如，在列举一系列信息时，译员可以使用先译出重要信息，后用"等等"的方式加以省略，并适时提醒听众哪些信息可以在屏幕上或者会议资料中找到。

在英译汉时，如果讲话人提到某个姓名，译员很难在极短的时间内记住或记录下全名，特别是音节较多的比较陌生的英文姓名；如果姓名前后还冠有头衔，并且比较难翻译时，在这种情况下，译员可以只翻译姓，略去名。

10.2.4 语言功能对等

语言是文化的载体，文化差异不像句子结构那样一目了然，它通常隐含在表面文字之下，成为口译交际中的一个盲点。如果译员只注意到语言表达的语法正确性，未能从原则上符合语言的社会文化功能，稍一疏忽就容易出差错，使双方无法达到交流的目的。例如，中方主人在机场迎接外方客人时会说："欢迎，欢迎！您一路上辛苦了！"若直译成"Welcome! You must be tired after a long journey."，虽然语法正确、内容准确，但语言功能方面的效果却相差甚远。按其语言功能，在接机时说这样一句话，无外乎是寒暄、问候，此时应翻译成"Did you have a pleasant journey?""Did you enjoy your trip?""How was your trip?"会更得体，更符合语言的社会文化功能。这样的例子不胜枚举。送客人时，主人会说："请慢走"，客人会说"请留步"。译员在英译的时候，不能直译，而要根据其语言功能，译成"Thank you for coming. See you next time!""Thank you for your hospitality. See you!"等。所以，对于隐含在表层语言背后的文化背景，译员需要进行细致地理解和分析，并根据其语言功能进行意义重组，适当调整用词与表达，以便双方达到交流、沟通的目的。

10.2.5 禁忌话题处理

英汉文化差异还体现在禁忌话题方面。西方人注重个体、个性和个人隐私，诸如党派的立场与观点、宗教、年龄、婚姻状况、收入情况、个人关系等属于极为隐私的话题，公开谈论是西方人的禁忌之一。对于上述绝大部分内容，中国人并没有严格的忌讳。在中国文化中，有些话题却是缄口不语的，如生病和死亡是人们最忌讳、最不愿谈论的话题，他们在谈话中会刻意回避"病""伤""死"等字眼。另外，"性"在中国是一个十分隐秘的话题。中国人以性观念、性道德保守而著称，汉语中有关"性"的表达几乎无一不采用委婉的形式。

同一话题，在一种文化中是无伤大雅的，在另一种文化中可能就不大得体，甚至可能使双方陷入不必要的尴尬之中。在口译时，如果出现敏感话题，译员需要懂得变通。例如，中文里有这样的恭维："您年纪这么大，身体还是这么健康。"但在英语文化里，人们忌讳直接说对方年纪大，因此不能译成"You are old but still look so healthy."。这样不但没有丝毫赞美之意，反而把别人给得罪了，所以可以译成"You look great."或"You look wonderful."。"你每月挣多少钱"恐怕是西方人最忌讳的私人问题了。若遇到这种情况，译员可以把直接问题变为间接问题，不针对个人，而是针对一个群体。若对方是销售经理，可以说"How much does a sales manager make a year？"或"What is the national average salary for a sales manager？"。如果遇到类似"您是支持工党还是保守党"的话题，译员不妨转移话题为"Which Party will win the election in your opinion？"。

10.3 医疗卫生口译

10.3.1 医疗卫生译前准备

A. 词汇

- 公共卫生：public health
- 卫生保健：health care
- 卫生机构：health institution
- 医疗物资：medical supplies
- 医疗机构：medical institution
- 医疗人员：medical personnel / health workforce / health workers
- 医疗保险：medical insurance
- 定点医院：designated hospital
- 发热门诊：fever clinic
- 重症监护病房：intensive care unit (ICU)
- 流行病学：epidemiology

第十章 口译的应变策略

- 疫情 / 流行病：epidemic
- 大流行疫情 / 疾病：pandemic
- 传染病：communicable disease
- 新冠肺炎（新型冠状病毒肺炎）：COVID-19 (coronavirus disease 2019)
- 呼吸道疾病（呼吸系统疾病）：respiratory disease
- 肺炎：pneumonia
- 病原体：pathogen
- 基因序列：genetic sequence
- 发病率：morbidity
- 死亡率：mortality rate
- 致病性：pathogenicity
- 传染性：transmissibility/infectivity
- 人传人：person-to-person/human-to-human transmission
- 潜伏期：incubation/latent period
- 病毒携带者：virus carrier
- 无症状感染者：asymptomatic carrier
- 密切接触者：close contact
- 超级传播者：super spreader
- 飞沫传播：droplet transmission
- 易感人群：susceptible/vulnerable population
- 核酸检测：nucleic acid test
- 检测能力：testing capacity
- 医学观察：medical observation/watch
- 确诊 / 重症 / 死亡 / 治愈出院 / 疑似病例：confirmed/severe/fatal/cured and discharged/suspected cases

- 免疫：immunity
- 疫苗：vaccine
- 应对疫情：respond to/contain/fight/tackle the epidemic
- 疫情防控：epidemic prevention and control
- 诊断、治疗、追踪和筛查：diagnosis, treatment, tracing, and screening
- 早发现、早报告、早隔离、早治疗：the early detection, reporting, quarantine, and treatment
- （公共场所）消毒、通风以及体温检测：disinfection, ventilation, and body temperature monitoring (in public areas)
- 药店：pharmacy/drugstore
- 呼吸机：ventilator
- 防护服：protective gown
- 护目镜：goggles
- 口罩：mask
- 青蒿素：qinghaosu/artemisinin
- 国家卫生健康委员会（国家卫健委）：National Health Commission (NHC)
- 国家医疗保障局：National Healthcare Security Administration (NHSA)
- 中国疾病预防控制中心（中国疾控中心）：Chinese Center for Disease Control and Prevention (China CDC)
- 《国际卫生条例》：International Health Regulations (IHR)
- 《本草纲目》：*Compendium of Materia Media*
- 英国国家医疗服务体系：National Health Service (NHS) in England

B. 背景知识

- 世界卫生组织：World Health Organization (WHO)

  The WHO is a specialized agency of the United Nations responsible for international public health. The WHO Constitution, which establishes the agency's governing structure and principles, states its main objective as "the attainment by all peoples of the highest possible level of health". It is headquartered in Geneva, Switzerland, with 6 semi-autonomous regional offices and 150 field offices worldwide. The current WHO Director-General is Dr. Tedros Adhanom Ghebreyesus.

The principle that all people should enjoy the highest standard of health, regardless of race, religion, political belief, economic or social condition, has guided WHO's work for the past 70 years, since it was first set up as the lead agency for international health in the new United Nations system.

- 世界卫生日: World Health Day

The World Health Day is a global health awareness day celebrated every year on April 7, under the sponsorship of the WHO, as well as other related organizations. It is one of eight official global health campaigns marked by the WHO, along with World Tuberculosis Day, World Immunization Week, World Malaria Day, World No Tobacco Day, World AIDS Day, World Blood Donor Day, and World Hepatitis Day.

- 公共卫生: public health

Public health has been defined as "the science and art of preventing disease", prolonging life, and improving quality of life through organized efforts and informed choices of society, organizations, public and private communities, and individuals. Analyzing the determinants of health of a population and the threats it faces is the basis for public health. The "public" can be as small as a handful of people or as large as a village or an entire city; in the case of a pandemic, it may encompass several continents. The concept of "health" takes physical, psychological, and social well-being into account. As such, according to the WHO, it is not merely the absence of disease or infirmity and more recently, a resource for everyday living.

- 公共卫生基础设施: public health infrastructure

Public health infrastructure, referred to as the nerve center of the public health system, provides the capacity to prevent disease, promote health, and prepare for and respond to both acute threats and chronic challenges to health. A strong public health infrastructure includes a capable and qualified workforce, up-to-date data and information systems, and agencies that can assess and respond to public health needs. It provides the necessary foundation for undertaking the basic responsibilities of public health.

- 国际关注的突发公共卫生事件: Public Health Emergency of International Concern (PHEIC)

A Public Health Emergency of International Concern is a formal declaration by the WHO of "an extraordinary event which is determined to constitute a public health risk to other states through the international spread of disease and to potentially require a coordinated international response", formulated when a situation arises that is "serious, sudden, unusual, or unexpected", which "carries implications for public health beyond the affected state's national border" and "may require immediate international action". Under the 2005 International Health Regulations, states have a legal duty to respond promptly to a PHEIC.

10.3.2 医疗卫生连续、交替口译

课堂练习：口译下列语段，注意所学口译技巧的应用。

练习一　视译

1) At present, 7,000 NHS Chinese medical workers are fighting shoulder to

shoulder with their British colleagues. Chinese communities in this country are working actively to donate funds and supplies to the NHS. Businesses from our two countries are also collecting supplies and raising funds through various channels. Today, we are here to witness the donation of the first shipment of medical supplies from the China Chamber of Commerce in the U.K. and the Bank of China to the City of London. These supplies, including ventilators, protective gowns, goggles, masks, and gloves, will be sent to NHS hospitals and health care institutions in the very front line in a timely manner. This donation, once again, shows the global vision of Chinese businesses that are willing to live up to their social responsibilities. It demonstrates true friendship between China and the U.K. in times of hardship.

2) China values social stability and understands that inclusive social services, also for health, contribute to social cohesion and stability. Over the last decade, China embarked on the biggest health system reform the world has ever seen, aiming to extend health services beyond the country's prosperous urban centers. At the start of the century, less than one third of China's population had access to health insurance. Now nearly 100% do. This equality in access to health services underpins social harmony. In essence, China has given its huge population a safety net that protects people from being impoverished by the costs of health care. This makes a tremendous contribution to a fair and prosperous society.

3) 今天的中国与70年前的中国完全不可同日而语，因为中国人民的健康状况已显著改善。"人生七十古来稀"，这句古话放在今天的中国早已不适用了。作为衡量经济社会发展水平和医疗卫生服务水平的综合指标，中国人民的人均寿命在70年间实现巨大跨越：从1949年的35岁到2020年的77岁。这主要得益于：目标明确的公共卫生运动降低了婴儿及儿童死亡率以及减少了传染病，经济状况的改善有助于营养、教育和卫生服务资源分配的改善。现在，中国人民比70年前活得更长寿、更健康。

4）中医药发祥于中华大地，在不断汲取世界文明成果的同时，它不断丰富与发展自己，并逐步传播到世界各地。早在秦汉时期，中医药就传播到周边国家，并对这些国家的传统医药产生重大影响。预防天花的种痘技术在明清时代就传遍世界。《本草纲目》被翻译成多种文字并广为流传，达尔文称之为"中国古代的百科全书"。针灸的神奇疗效引发全球持续的针灸热。抗疟疾药物"青蒿素"的发明拯救了全球数百万人的生命，特别是发展中国家。

练习二　听译（1—4）

课堂练习：听下列录音，进行连续口译。

练习三　WHO Director-General's Opening Remarks at High-Level Video Conference on Belt and Road International Cooperation

小组练习：三人一组，分别担任记者、被采访人和口译员，进行交替口译练习。练习时注意转换角色。

练习四　中国驻英国大使刘晓明接受英国广播公司《尖锐对话》栏目专访[1]

背景知识

2020年4月28日，中国驻英国大使刘晓明接受英国广播公司（BBC）《尖锐对话》栏目资深主持人斯蒂芬·萨克在线专访，就中国抗击新冠

---

[1] 来自中国驻英国大使馆网站。

第十章 口译的应变策略

> 肺炎疫情阐明立场，澄清事实，激浊扬清。
>
> 新冠肺炎疫情是指由新型冠状病毒（COVID-19），即严重急性呼吸系统综合征冠状病毒 2（SARS-CoV-2）所引发的肺炎疫情。2019 年末始发，随后在 2020 年初迅速扩散至全球多国，逐渐演变成一场全球性大瘟疫，被多个国际组织及媒体形容为自第二次世界大战以来全球面临的最严峻危机。截至 2021 年 2 月 3 日，全球新冠肺炎累计确诊近 1.04 亿例，死亡超 224 万例。

Sackur: Ambassador Liu Xiaoming, welcome to *HARDtalk*.

刘大使： 谢谢！很高兴再次见到你。

Sackur: We are delighted to have you on our program at this difficult time. Let me start actually with a very simple, direct question: Do you accept that COVID-19 has its origins in China?

刘大使： 病毒最早发现于武汉并不等于起源于武汉。根据多方信息，包括 BBC 的报道，病毒可能源自任何地方，甚至在航空母舰或潜艇中可以找到，在一些与中国很少联系的国家中可以找到，在从未去过中国的人群中也可以找到。所以我们不能说它源自中国。

Sackur: I'm a little confused by that answer. Clearly, it is a new virus. It originated somewhere. It seems that, according to all of the immunologists and virologists, it crossed from animals to humans. And there was a first case and then it spread. There is no doubt that the first case was in China. I'm wondering why you are telling me that it spread all over the world and people who caught it had never been to China. That is clear because it has become a pandemic. But the question that matters so much is: Where did it start?

刘大使： 我认为这个问题应交由科学家来解答。据我了解，中国的首起病例是由张继先医生于 2019 年 12 月 27 日向中国地方卫生主管部门报告的。我还看到报道称中国以外有些病例甚至远早于此。昨天英国报纸上的报道称，英国的科学家、医学专家在去年早些时候就曾警告政府，可能存在一种未知病毒。因此，我只能说中国第一例报告的病例于2019年12月27日发生在武汉。

Sackur: I think there's no doubt that experts believe the origin of the first outbreak, first examples of this COVID-19 virus to be found in human beings, came from Wuhan and the surrounding area in China. I just wonder whether you accept that it is very important that we understand exactly what happened at the beginning of this outbreak, and that we understand frankly what mistakes and missteps were made, which allowed the first outbreak to become a global pandemic.

刘大使： 我认为这仍待商榷，我们得承认有不同看法。病毒是在中国武汉首次发现的，但不能说它起源于武汉。让我给你介绍一下中国抗疫时间表。张继先医生首先于2019年12月27日上报了不明原因肺炎病例。中国卫生部门和疾控中心在四天后，也就是12月31日以最快的时间通知了世界卫生组织，并与其他国家共享这一信息。中国还第一时间同世界卫生组织分享病原体，在第一时间同世界卫生组织和其他国家分享病毒基因序列。

Sackur: Ambassador, let me just interrupt you on this question of timeline because you missed out one very important point. On December 30, a doctor in Wuhan, Li Wenliang, used his chat group online to tell fellow doctors that there was a new and very worrying disease in Wuhan. He advised his colleagues that they must wear protective clothing to avoid this new infection. And just a couple of days later, he was summoned to the public security bureau. He was made to sign a letter in which he confessed to making false statements that had severely disturbed the social order. That was the beginning of an official cover-up, which continued through the month of January.

刘大使： 现在我明白为什么一些人要鼓吹进行所谓的独立调查了，其实就是试图罗织借口来批评中国掩盖真相。但事实是，李文亮不是

第十章 口译的应变策略

"吹哨者",正如我刚才说的,张继先医生比李文亮早三天向卫生部门报告,武汉市卫生部门随即向中央政府报告。四天后,也就是李文亮发出微信信息后一天,中国政府与世卫组织及其他国家共享了这一信息。完全不存在所谓的掩盖事实。

Sackur: With respect, Mr. Ambassador, the information that was shared was actually extremely limited. Because on January 14, we now know this from the leaks that have been given to the *Washington Post* and the Associated Press; we know that internally the head of China's National Health Commission, Mr. Ma Xiaowei, laid out a very grim assessment of what was happening. He said that the situation was severe. Complex, clustered cases suggest human-to-human transmission is happening, the memo said. The risk of transmission and spread is high; that was internal. But in public, the head of China's Disease Control Emergency Center, the very next day, said that the risk of sustained human-to-human transmission is low; that it was preventable and controllable. So, I put it to you again: There is compelling evidence that China for weeks did not tell the truth.

刘大使: 你都没有给我足够的时间回答问题,我还没有答完关于李文亮的问题。所谓的"掩盖事实"是不存在的。张医生通过正常渠道向卫生部门报告,但李文亮则在朋友圈传播相关信息。在任何国家,如果出现极其危险的未知病毒等情况,都可能引起恐慌。我认为警方传唤李医生,向他提出警告,要求他停止网上传播,这不能称为"隐瞒"。疫情已经通过正规渠道上报,这种情况下要尽量避免恐慌。目前,英国政府也在打击利用假消息制造恐慌以达到个人目的的做法。有关李文亮医生的事已经有结论,中央政府接到报告后,立即向武汉派出调查组,武汉市公安局决定撤销对李医生的训诫书。李医生被追认为烈士,被授予很高的荣誉。

Sackur: Dr. Li was in deed regarded by the Chinese people as a hero when he died.

刘大使：不仅是中国人民，中国政府也是一样，不能区别开来。

Sackur: With respect, I think the people of China are very aware, and I come back to it, that the Chinese government wasn't straight with them, nor with the outside world. Just tell me, if you can one more time, why on January 14 was the National Health Commission document—that was an internal document—labeled not to be spread on the Internet, not to be publicly disclosed, in which it said that there was evidence of human-to-human transmission, clustered cases, severe and complex problem?

刘大使：我想你们的所有信息都来自《华盛顿邮报》，你们过于依赖美国媒体。我衷心希望你们能使用世界卫生组织的信息。我们与世界卫生组织分享了所有信息。我看了你对世界卫生组织新冠特使纳巴罗（David Nabarro）博士的专访，中国始终坚持公开、透明的原则，第一时间与世界卫生组织分享信息。一方面在中国国内，我们必须保持高度警惕，采取最严格的防控措施，当时对这个病毒并不十分了解，不知道未来会发生什么。另一方面我们与世界卫生组织和其他国家分享了信息和我们对病毒的认知。

Sackur: But Ambassador, with all respect, your problem is—you're a very senior diplomat and you know this is a problem—that many people around the world simply don't believe the Chinese version of events. Donald Trump, only a few hours ago, said that he is not happy at all with China's stance. "They could have stopped the virus at the source," he said, "We are undertaking a thorough investigation." And the Vice President Mike Pence has listed a whole host of reasons why the United States believes that China was not straight with the world and is therefore culpable for the fact that this pandemic is now causing so much death and so much economic damage right around the world. You have, as China, a massive problem now.

刘大使：我不同意这种说法。相反，一些西方国家正面临更大的困难。疫情发生后，中国第一时间与世界卫生组织和其他国家通力合作，

第十章 口译的应变策略

我们向 150 多个国家派出技术援助和医疗专家组,并提供医疗物资援助,因此受到这些国家的高度评价。我认为,美国不能代表全世界,因为不少西方国家,包括英国、法国、德国,也对中国表示赞赏。你引用了特朗普总统的表态,我也想引用几句他有关中国的表态。1月24日,在中国通报疫情大约一个月之后,特朗普总统表示"美国高度赞赏中国的努力和透明度"。六天之后,他表示"中国人民付出许多,我们正在与中国紧密合作"。二月初,他又表示"习近平主席工作出色、疫情处理得很好"。

Sackur: Things have changed a great deal since the end of January. You say, look at what we've done to deliver medical assistance and equipment around the world. What many people see is China running a campaign of disinformation and propaganda around the world in recent weeks. You say, we have a great relationship with France. The French just called in your counterpart, the Chinese Ambassador in France, accusing him of spreading disinformation because the Embassy website in Paris is claiming that old people in care homes in France are being abandoned to suffer and die alone. That's a colleague of yours. Another colleague of yours in the Ministry of Foreign Affairs uses social media to promote the conspiracy theory that the U.S. military has smuggled coronavirus into China. Why is your country running this disinformation campaign?

刘大使: 我认为你选错了目标。不是中国在散布假消息。如果将中国领导人、中国外交官和中国大使的表态与美国领导人、美国外交官和美国大使做一个比较,你就会发现谁在散布假消息。

Sackur: Do you agree with Zhao Lijian, the spokesman of the Ministry of Foreign Affairs, who did put up the link suggesting that the U.S. military has smuggled coronavirus into China? Is that something that you also believe?

刘大使: 赵是转推一些媒体的报道。我不明白你为什么抓住中国某个人的言论不放,却对美国国家领导人、高级官员,特别是美国最高级别外交官、国务卿发布的假消息视而不见？只要谈到中国，他们就没有好话；中国在抗疫斗争中向美国伸出援手，结果却成了恶人。我实在不能理解。

Sackur: In your view, Ambassador, how deep is the crisis with the United States right now, that has been sparked by all of the accusations that have arisen from the coronavirus? How deep is the diplomatic crisis?

刘大使：中方当然希望与美国保持良好关系。我曾两次常驻美国，我始终相信中美和则两利、斗则俱伤，我们有充分的理由与美方保持良好关系，但这应该建立在相互信任、合作而不对抗的基础上，双方需要相向而行。疫情发生以来，习近平主席和特朗普总统保持密切沟通，通了两次电话，讨论国际抗疫合作。我想强调的是，中国不是美国的敌人，新冠病毒才是，美国应该找对目标。

Sackur: It's a very important message you're sending. Maybe China could consider some gestures that would improve relations with not just the United States but many other countries, including Australia and the U.K., who've made the same point to your government.

One, will you now categorically guarantee to close down the so-called "wet markets" that there will no longer be the sale of these live wild animals in the food markets? Is that now something that has been banned, not just in the short term, but absolutely banned forever in China?

刘大使：首先，我不同意你关于中国与许多国家关系出现问题的说法，中国的朋友多，对手少，敌人更少。正如我所说，少数西方国家不能代表整个世界。中国拥有良好的对外关系，正在积极推动国际抗疫合作。正如习近平主席所说，团结合作是国际社会战胜疫情最有力武器。

Sackur: Ambassador, we are short of time. I just need specific answer on the "wet markets". Are they right now closed for good, yes or no?

刘大使：事实上，中国根本不存在所谓的"湿货市场"，这个说法对很多中国人来说很陌生，是一种西方的、外来的说法。人们常说的是农贸市场和活禽海鲜市场，主要销售新鲜的蔬菜、海鲜等农副产品，也有少数市场销售活禽。你所谈到的应该是非法销售野生动物的市场，这已经被彻底禁止。中国已经通过法律，全面禁止非法野生动物交易。

Sackur: That is therefore a recognition—I just want to be clear—a recognition on your government's part of the dangers of those markets, where live wild animals were sold alongside other food stuff; they were dangers that did cause the spread coronavirus from animals to humans.

刘大使：我们终于达成了一项一致。请注意，这里所说的是非法野生动物市场已完全被禁止，在中国猎捕、交易、食用野生动物都是非法的。

Sackur: So people watching this will only wish that you had made that ban real before the coronavirus has spread and caused such terrible damage around the world. Are you in any way prepared to say sorry for what has happened?

刘大使：你又回到了采访开始时的问题。我要说，不能因为疫情在中国发现就指责中国，这是错误的。中国发现了疫情，在很多与中国毫无联系的地方也发现了疫情。不能因为中方暴发疫情就指责中国，要看到中国竭尽所能努力抗疫。中国是病毒受害者，中国不是病毒制造者，中国也不是病毒源头。对于这一点，必须要明确。

Sackur: China is seen, for example, by leading politicians in this country, like the Chairman of the Parliamentary Foreign Affairs Select Committee, as very much the cause. He's talked about a Soviet-style system, a toxic system, inside your government, inside your regime, which he says has been responsible for not just betraying the Chinese people and their health or well-being, but betraying the wider world as well. And there are now calls in the United Kingdom, and also calls in the United States and other countries, for a disengagement from close economic ties with China. In Britain, it's of course centered on Huawei, your telephones giant's activities in the 5G sector. People say that it should no longer be tolerated in the United Kingdom. As the Ambassador in the U.K., are you worried that there is going to be an economic disengagement?

刘大使：既担心，也不担心。你谈到的那位政界要员，他的观点不能代表英国政府的官方立场。我相信，在约翰逊首相的领导下，英国政府仍致力于发展强劲的中英关系。在与习主席的两次通话中，约翰逊首相重申将致力于推进中英关系"黄金时代"。疫情期间，中英除了紧密沟通之外，还积极开展合作。我出任中国驻英国大使10年了，从未见过两国领导人和高层保持如此密切的联系，除了习近平主席与约翰逊首相的两次通话外，国务委员兼外交部长王毅、中央外事工作委员会办公室主任杨洁篪分别同英国外交大臣拉布、英国首相国家安全事务顾问塞德维尔保持密切沟通，我也与卫生大臣汉考克，商业、能源和产业战略大臣夏尔马，以及外交大臣拉布保持密切接触。以上表明中英关系十分强劲。至于你提到有人将中国比作苏联，这完全是"冷战"思维。我们已经生活在21世纪第三个十年，而这些人还停留在过去"冷战"时期。中国不是苏联。中英之间的共同利益远大于分歧，我对中英关系充满信心。

Sackur: All right, Ambassador, we have to end there. But I do thank you very much indeed for joining me on *HARDtalk* at this difficult time. Liu Xiaoming, thank you very much indeed.

刘大使：不必客气。

参考文献

Anderson, J. R. (2014). *Cognitive psychology and its implications* (8th ed.). San Francisco: Freeman.

Bachman, L. F. (1990). *Fundamental considerations in language testing.* Oxford: Oxford University Press.

Bachman, L. F. & Palmer, A. S. (1996). *Language testing in practice.* Oxford: Oxford University Press.

Baker, M. (2011). *In other words: A course book on translation* (2nd ed.). London & New York: Routledge.

Cokely, D. (1992). *Interpretation: A sociolinguistic model.* Burtonsville, MD: Linstok Press.

Cynthia, B. R. (unknown publication date). *Advances in teaching sign language interpreters.* Retrieved from Gallaudet University Press website.

Gile, D. (2009). *Basic concepts and models for interpreter and translator training* (2nd ed.). Amsterdam: John Benjamins.

Gillies, A. (2013). *Conference interpreting—A student's practice book.* London & New York: Routledge.

Grice, H. P. (1975). *Logic and conversation.* New York: Academic Press.

Jones, R. (2002). *Conference interpreting explained.* Manchester: St. Jerome Publishing.

Jones, R. (2008). *Conference interpreting explained.* Shanghai: Shanghai Foreign Language Education Press.

Pochhacker, F. (2010). *Introducing interpreting studies*. Beijing: Foreign Language Teaching and Research Press.

Pöchhacker, F. (2019). *Routledge encyclopedia of interpreting studies*. London & New York: Routledge.

Roy, C. B. (1950). *Interpreting as a discourse process*. Oxford: Oxford University Press.

Seleskovitch, D. (1998). *Interpreting for international conferences*. Washington, DC: Pen and Booth.

Seleskovitch, D. (2002). Language and memory: A study of note-taking in consecutive interpreting. In F. Pöchhacker & S. Miriam (Eds.), *The interpreting studies reader* (pp.121–129). London & New York: Routledge.

Setton, R. (1999). *Simultaneous interpretation: A Cognitive-pragmatic analysis*. Amsterdam & Philadelphia, PA: John Benjamins.

Setton, R. (2011). *Interpreting Chinese, interpreting China*. Amsterdam: John Benjamins.

Setton, R. & Dawrant A. (2016). *Conference interpreting—A trainer's guide*. Amsterdam: John Benjamins.

鲍刚.2005.口译理论概述.北京：中国对外翻译出版有限公司．

陈胜白.2013.口译研究的生态学途径.上海：复旦大学出版社．

崔校平.2015.英语词汇与西方文化.北京：清华大学出版社．

李学兵.2005a.口译过程中影响理解的因素及理解能力的培训策略.外语教学,（5）：85—90.

李学兵.2005b.英语口译教学的目标与内容选择.北京第二外国语学院学报,（4）：76—80.

李学兵.2010.逻辑思维与口译理解.中国科技翻译,（8）：20—23.

李学兵.2012.如何在口译教学中培养学生的逻辑思维能力.外国语文,（7）：198—200.

刘和平. 2005. 口译理论与教学. 北京：中国对外翻译出版有限公司.

刘和平. 2001. 口译技巧—思维科学与口译推理教学法. 北京：中国对外翻译出版有限公司.

刘和平. 2017. 翻译学：口译理论和口译教育. 上海：复旦大学出版社.

刘宓庆. 2004. 口笔译理论研究. 北京：中国对外翻译出版有限公司.

梅德明. 2000. 高级口译教程. 北京：北京大学出版社.

任文. 2010. 联络口译过程中译员的主体性意识研究. 北京：外语教学与研究出版社.

王斌华. 2019. 口译理论研究. 北京：外语教学与研究出版社.

谢平. 2018. 探索大脑的终极秘密:学习、记忆、梦和意识. 北京:科学出版社.

许文胜. 2016. 大数据时代云端翻转课堂模式下的口译教学探索. 上海：同济大学出版社.

亚里士多德. 1992. 论记忆. 秦典华,译. 苗力田（主编）. 亚里士多德全集. 第六卷. 北京：中国人民大学出版社.

杨承淑. 2005. 口译教学研究. 北京：中国对外翻译出版有限公司.

中国外文出版发行事业局，中国翻译研究院，中国翻译协会. 2017. 中国关键词："一带一路"篇. 北京：新世界出版社.

钟述孔. 2001. 实用口译手册. 北京：中国对外翻译出版有限公司.

附录：口译音频实录

第二章　口译听辨理解与逻辑分析

练习三

孙悟空三打白骨精

故事线索

引子：人物——唐僧与徒弟孙悟空、猪八戒和沙僧去西天取经。

　　　地点——崇山峻岭间。

　　　铺垫——悟空火眼金睛，善识妖怪，除恶降魔，去寻找食物。

情节发展：1. 一打白骨精变的少女。

　　　　　2. 二打白骨精变的老太婆。

　　　　　3. 三打白骨精变的老公公。

高潮：悟空被赶走，唐僧被捉。悟空解救师傅。

结尾：白骨精变成一堆白骨。师徒一行继续西行。

练习四

莴苣姑娘（长发公主）

故事线索

引子：人物——一对夫妇等待孩子降生。

　　　铺垫——妻子想吃隔壁花园里的莴苣。

情节发展：1. 一次偷莴苣吃。

　　　　　　二次偷莴苣，巫婆出现，丈夫答应把初生儿送给巫婆。

女婴出生被抱走。

2. 女婴长成少女，被困在塔上。王子学巫婆上塔与少女相见。铺垫——约会，相爱，带丝绸。

3. 巫婆发现他们的恋情。

高潮：巫婆抓住王子，王子眼睛被玫瑰刺刺伤而失明。

结尾：王子找到女孩，眼睛复明，回到王国，幸福地生活在一起。

练习五

互联网发展

要点、思路

我国互联网发展呈现四个方面的新变化：

1. 信息形态方面，信息传播形式以文字为主向音频、视频、图片等多媒体形态转变。

2. 应用领域方面，从以信息传播和娱乐消费为主向商务服务领域延伸，互联网开始逐步深入到国民经济更深层次和更宽领域。

3. 服务模式方面，从提供信息服务向提供平台服务延伸。

4. 传播手段方面，传统互联网向移动互联网延伸，手机上网成为新潮流。

练习六

Education Revolutions

要点、思路

教育的四次革命：

1. The first education revolution. Organized learning. Necessary education.

2. The second education revolution, the coming of schools and universities.

Institutionalized education.

3. The third education revolution. Development of printing. Education for the masses.

4. The fourth education revolution. AI, the new way for spreading education across the world.

练习七

为中英教育交流合作增光添彩

要点、思路

"中英数学教师交流项目"的意义：

1. 促交流、拓合作的品牌项目。

2. 打基础、利长远的互惠平台。

3. 增互鉴、促了解的有益实践。

对该项目寄予的两点希望：

1. 相互学习，共同提高。

2. 教书育人，传承友谊。

练习八

The Importance of Studying Abroad

要点、思路

出国学习的重要性：

1. Studying abroad is not just an educational opportunity for students, but also a vital part of a country's foreign policy.

2. It is quickly becoming the key to success in global economy.

3. It's also about shaping the future of a country and of the world.

练习十

中英是"一带一路"的"天然合作伙伴"

中英是"一带一路"的"天然合作伙伴"。英国的经验、创意与中国的效率、市场化能力优势互补,"一带一路"倡议与"全球化英国"、英国现代化工业战略契合相通。英国还拥有英语语言、发达的国际金融业、成熟的法律和咨询服务、与沿线国家历史文化渊源深厚等独特优势,这些优势资源与"一带一路"建设需求高度契合。因此,中英"一带一路"合作潜力巨大,前景广阔。

练习十一

中国的消费能力和消费需求大幅提升

中国已经形成规模为4亿多的世界上最大的中等收入群体,其消费能力和消费需求大幅提升。举例来说,20世纪70年代,中国老百姓家庭的消费水平是百元级的,即"三转一响一咔嚓"——手表、缝纫机、自行车,收音机和照相机;到了80年代,家庭消费水平升级为千元级的,即"三机一箱"——电视机、洗衣机、录放机和电冰箱;到了90年代,家庭消费水平是万元级的,即"两电一调"——电脑、电话和空调;进入21世纪,中国百姓家庭消费水平晋升为十万到百万元级,消费水平以汽车、住房和旅游为代表。

练习十二

Trade and Economic Relations Between China and the U.S.

China is the world's biggest developing country and the United States is the biggest developed country. Trade and economic relations between China and the U.S. are of great significance for the two countries as well as for the stability and development of the world economy. Since the establishment of diplomatic relations, bilateral trade and economic ties between China and the U.S. have developed steadily. A close partnership has been forged under which interests of the two countries have become closer and wider. Both countries have benefited from this partnership, as has the rest of the world.

练习十三

China's Achievements in 40 Years of Reform and Opening-up

This year marks the 40th anniversary of China's reform and opening-up. Thanks to 40 years of persistent efforts, China has achieved the great leap from getting on its feet to becoming prosperous and strong. China is now the second largest economy in the world and it has lifted more than 700 million people out of poverty. The achievements are attributable to the strong leadership of the Communist Party of China, to the development path that suits China's national conditions, and to the hard efforts of the Chinese people. Today, the Chinese people are striding proudly towards the goal of building a moderately prosperous society and a great modern socialist country in all respects.

第三章　口译的短期记忆

练习一

天安门广场

现在我们来到了天安门广场，这是北京的中心。西面是人民大会堂；南面是毛主席纪念堂；东面是国家博物馆；中间是人民英雄纪念碑；北面是天安门。天安门原是明清两代皇城的正门，由此进入故宫。现在天安门是中华人民共和国的象征。

练习二

中国春节

在中国所有的传统节日中，春节是最重要、最热闹的节日。人们不管离家有多远，都要高高兴兴地赶回家与家人共度新年。为庆祝这一节日，家家户户都会提前大扫除、买年货、贴窗花以及做各种美食。到了年三十，大家都要穿上新衣服、贴春联、放鞭炮、吃年夜饭、守岁，辞旧迎新。大人还要把崭新的钱放在红包里，给孩子们发压岁钱。大年初一开始，人们还要走亲戚、互相拜年，祝愿新的一年一帆风顺、健康幸福。

练习三

The Giant Panda

The giant panda is a black and white bear that feeds on bamboo. It is easily recognized by the large, distinctive black patches around its eyes, over the ears, and across its round body. A panda is a cartoon image delicately designed by God. Its lovely chubby round face looks like a chubby child wearing sunglasses. Its two big round ears look like black velvet flowers atop its head. When observing the panda walking, you will find that its bottom is swinging—just like a fashion model on the T-shaped catwalk.

In the wild, giant pandas are found in thick bamboo forests, high up in the mountains of central China, mostly in Sichuan Province, but also in neighboring Gansu and Shaanxi Provinces. Panda's exact number in the wild is unknown, but scientists believe there are about 1,100 giant pandas remaining in the wild. As an ancient relic animal, it is regarded as a "national treasure" by the Chinese people, while the World Wildlife Fund takes it as a symbol of global nature protection.

练习四

Three Wishes

A farmer's wife spent most of her time wishing for the things which she did not have. She often said: "I wish I were rich," or "I wish I were beautiful," or "I wish I had a handsome husband."

One day, some fairies decided to permit her to have three wishes as an experiment. The farmer and his wife talked for a long time about what she should wish for. Suddenly the farmer's wife became a little hungry, and from the force of a habit she said: "I wish I had some sausages to eat." Immediately her plate on the table were full of sausages. Then an argument began because the farmer complained that his wife had wasted one of their good wishes on such a cheap thing as the sausages. The argument grew hotter, and finally the wife said angrily: "I wish the sausages were hanging from your nose." Immediately the sausages flew to her husband's nose, and there they remained.

There was only one thing the poor woman could do. She really loved her husband, so she had to use her third wish to remove the sausages from her husband's nose. So except for a few sausages, she got nothing from her three wishes.

练习五

孔子学院和孔子课堂

为什么孔子学院和孔子课堂在英国这么火？我想主要源自三大魅力。一是中华文明的魅力。中国有着5 000多年的悠久历史，中华文明生生不息，从未间断。学会中文就拿到了打开了解中华文明大门的"金钥匙"。二是"中国奇迹"的魅力。中国改革开放40年来，中国经济总量跃升至世界第二，7亿多人脱贫，为世界发展做出巨大贡献。学会中文就可以更好地了解"中国奇迹"背后的故事，更好地抓住"中国机遇"。三是"黄金时代"的魅力。2015年习近平主席成功对英国进行国事访问，开启中英关系"黄金时代"。两国各领域的交流合作不断提质增效，中文日益成为增进中英人民友谊的"黄金纽带"。

笔记示范

孔子学院和孔子课堂在英国火的原因：

1. 中华文明的魅力。5 000多年。

2. "中国奇迹"的魅力。经济总量世界第二，7亿多人脱贫。

3. "黄金时代"的魅力。2015年习主席访英，交流不断，中文成为纽带。

练习六

沉迷网络游戏的危害

玩网络游戏是一种常见的娱乐方式,适度地玩网络游戏有益身心,但是如果沉迷其中不能自拔,则危害极大。首先,沉迷网络游戏会影响学业。很多学生一旦沉迷网络游戏,就对其他一切事情漠不关心,全身心都投入游戏中,甚至为了玩网络游戏而逃课,从而导致他们的学业出现问题。同时,这些学生是在虚度人生最美好的时光。在人生最美好的时候不选择奋斗,而是沉迷网络游戏,以后事业无成的时候,他们肯定追悔莫及。其次,长时间玩网络游戏会损害身体健康。很多青少年玩网络游戏经常"废寝忘食",整天面对电脑坐着,长时间不动,这不但会导致近视、缺少睡眠,而且还会产生其他身体亚健康问题,如肥胖、心血管疾病、肠胃不适等。最后,沉迷网络游戏会影响一个人的心理健康。沉迷网络游戏后,人会很少跟身边的人沟通,长此以往,就会形成孤僻的性格,不愿与外界接触。有的网络游戏十分血腥、暴力,人一旦沉迷其中,自己的心理健康也会逐渐受到影响,甚至出现暴力倾向。沉迷网络游戏无法自拔,既虚度时光,又造成亚健康问题,极有可能会影响人的一生。

笔记示范

沉迷网络游戏的危害:

1. 影响学业,其他漠不关心,逃课,虚度时光。

2. 损害身体健康,近视、少眠、亚健康。

3. 出现心理问题,性格孤僻、暴力倾向。

练习七

The Benefits of Part-Time Jobs for College Students

There are many benefits for college students to do part-time jobs. One obvious reason is that they could finance part of their education, easing the financial burden on their parents. Earning their own spending money in this way may help them pay for books, special courses, clubs, etc. Second, students who work part-time may develop better time management skills. Going to classes, after-school studying, and working make for a busy schedule. It will take a lot of efforts to balance all of their projects and term papers in between shifts at the part-time jobs and hanging out with their friends. They tend to be better planners as they need to make sure they complete every task before the deadline. Third, a part-time job may help the students gain experience in the workplace that will be attractive to future employers after graduation. Even students who work in places not connected to their majors will look more impressive to potential employers. They will have some kind of work experience on their résumés to start and show prospective employers that they are dedicated and responsible. Fourth, students in part-time employment would have a chance of meeting different people, which would help them to become mature when dealing with interpersonal relationships. Employers look for employees who understand the work environment and work well as part of a team. Having a part-time job shows that the student is at least somewhat accustomed to the professional world, which will make the transition much easier. In a word, students should be encouraged to take up part-time employment outside school hours.

笔记示范

大学生做兼职工作的好处：

1. Financing part of their education.

2. Developing better time management skills.

3. Gaining experience in the workplace.

4. Becoming mature when dealing with interpersonal relationships.

练习八

The Education System in the U.K.

The education system in the U.K. is divided into four main parts: primary education, secondary education, further education, and higher education. Children in the U.K. have to legally attend primary and secondary education which run from about 5 years old until the student is 16 years old. Primary education begins at age 5 and continues until age 11, comprising key stages one and two under the U.K. educational system. From age 11 to 16, students will enter secondary school for key stages three and four and start their move towards taking the GCSE. Once students finish secondary education have they the option to extend into further education such as A-Levels or other such qualifications. Students planning to go to college or university must complete further education. The U.K. has a vast variety of higher education opportunities to provide students with over 100 universities offering various degree programs for students from the U.K. and around the world. In the U.K., about one third of all students go on to some form of higher education.

笔记示范

英国的教育体系：

1. Primary education：5~11 岁，一、二阶段。

2. Secondary education：11~16 岁，三、四阶段，GCSE 考试。

3. Further education：A-levels。

4. Higher education：100 多所大学，三分之一上大学。

练习九

寄语中国留学生

同学们，十九大报告在最后部分专门对青年提出了殷切希望："青年一代有理想、有本领、有担当，国家就有前途，民族就有希望。中国梦是历史的、现实的，也是未来的；是我们这一代的，更是青年一代的。中华民族伟大复兴的中国梦终将在一代代青年的接力奋斗中变为现实。"我们这一代人一定会完成好自己的历史使命，也为你们将要承担的使命感到骄傲，相信你们在新的征程上一定能够跑得更好、更快。

在这里，我也提几点希望。首先希望大家学业有成。要利用在这里学习的机会，认真研究和学习美国一切值得我们学习和借鉴的东西，这不仅包括自然科学技术，也包括社会科学、人文艺术等各个方面。美国值得我们学习的地方有很多，希望大家把它研究透、学到手。第二，希望大家广交朋友。中美两国人民可以说有一千个一万个应成为好朋友的理由，没有一个要成为敌人的理由。在美国人眼里，每一个中国留学生都是中国的形象大使，是美国人了解中国的一个窗户。希望你们跟美国同学和老师，跟美国人民广泛接触，让他们更多、更好、更真实地了解中国，了解中国人，了解中国的历史、文化和未来。第三，希望大家保重身体，注意安全。当前，美国社会特别是校园中恶性案件时有发生，希望大家注意人身安全，让你们在国内的家人放心。

最后，再次祝大家在新的一年里学业有成、身体健康、阖家欢乐！

笔记示范

对中国留学生提出的几点希望：

1. 学业有成。

2. 广交朋友。

3. 保重身体，注意安全。

练习十

"一带一路"倡议为何受到国际社会普遍欢迎？

"一带一路"倡议能够在短短4年时间里广受欢迎、深得人心，有多方面原因：

一是引领时代潮流，提供新发展"良方"。新形势下，世界经济仍面临较大的不确定性，和平赤字、发展赤字、治理赤字等挑战日益突出。不少人将上述挑战归咎于经济全球化，出现了"逆全球化"、保护主义甚至"贸易战"等论调。"一带一路"倡议,聚焦发展这个根本性问题,不仅推动经济全球化向更加包容普惠的方向发展,也为维护地区及世界的和平与稳定创造有利条件。从这个意义上讲,"一带一路"倡议是中国为经济全球化开出的一剂"良方",为世界经济企稳向好、可持续发展提供了正确答案和有效路径。

二是符合各方利益,造福全球民众。"一带一路"是从人类命运共同体的视角出发,倡导共商、共建、共享的合作理念,通过政策沟通、设施联通、贸易畅通、资金融通、民心相通实现各国共同发展和进步。"一带一路"把欧亚大陆两端,即发达的欧洲经济圈和充满活力的东亚经济圈紧密相连,推动构建公正、合理、透明的国际经贸投资规则体系,促进生产要素有序流动、资源高效配置、市场深度融合,让更多国家和民众体会到实实在在的"获得感"。

三是彰显强大包容性,实现合作共赢目标。"一带一路"传承和发扬丝路精神,蕴含着"和而不同""兼收并蓄"等东方智慧,充分照顾各参与方的舒适度和合理关切,通过加强发展战略对接,促进互联互通,实现地区经济融合发展,把共同利益的蛋糕做大。"一带一路"版权虽属中国,但欢迎各国广泛参与,收益为各国共享。通过"一带一路"建设,中国把自身发展同沿线各国繁荣更加紧密地结合起来,使中国倡导的合作共赢理念更好地落到实处。

笔记示范

"一带一路"倡议受到国际社会普遍欢迎的原因:

1. 引领时代潮流,提供新发展"良方"。
2. 符合各方利益,造福全球民众。
3. 彰显强大包容性,实现合作共赢目标。

练习十一

Should a Person Own a Car?

Should a person own a car? This is an important question. In a large urban area, there are some good reasons for owning a car. First, a car allows a person to move around freely. With a car, there is no need to check a bus schedule or wait for a train. Second, a car is a comfortable way to travel, especially in the wintertime. In bad weather, the driver stays warm and dry, while the poor bus or train rider might have to stand in the rain. Finally, a driver is usually safe in a car at night. The rider might need to walk down a dark street to get to a stop, or wait on a dark corner.

There are, on the other hand, many good reasons against owning a car. First, it can be very expensive. The price of fuel continues to rise and car insurance can cost 2,000~3,000 dollars a year. In addition, it is expensive to maintain and repair a car. A simple turn-up can cost $50. In an urban area, it might also be expensive to park the car. Second, owning a car can cause worry and stress. It is exhausting to drive in rush-hour traffic, or to drive around and around looking for a parking space. If you leave your car on the street, it might get stolen. That is something else to worry about. Finally, everyone needs to think about pollution and energy problems. Air pollution and noise pollution increase as more and more people drive cars. More and more cars also burn more and more fuel. At present, drivers may have to wait in long lines at filling stations in order to buy a couple of gallons of gasoline.

Should a person own a car? In order to answer the question, a person must weigh both sides. On the one hand, there is freedom of movement, comfort, and safety. On the other hand, there is expense, worry, and concern for the quality of life. For many people in large cities, the reasons against owning a car outweigh the reasons for owning a car. Therefore, the answer is negative: A person should not own a car.

笔记示范

1. 拥有一辆车的好处：

A. Freedom to move around.

B. Comfort to travel.

C. Safety at night.

2. 拥有一辆车的坏处：

A. Expenses.

    a. The price of fuel.

    b. The car insurance.

    c. Maintaining and repairing a car.

    d. Parking fee.

B. Worry and stress.

    a. Driving in rush-hour traffic.

    b. Looking for a parking space.

    c. Worrying the car being stolen.

C. Pollution and energy problem.

    a. Air and noise pollution.

    b. Fuel shortage.

3. 结论：人们不应该买车。

练习十二

Chinese New Year Greetings from the British Ambassador to China[1]

British Embassy in China; February 8, 2021

Hello! I'm Caroline Wilson, the British Ambassador to China. The Spring Festival is the most important festival for people in China and Chinese communities around the world, and I'm very excited to celebrate here this year, as this is my first Chinese New Year since I became the Ambassador to China. It's a time to celebrate, it's a time to reflect on the past year, and it's also a time to look ahead to the year ahead.

1　From British Embassy in China website.

I'm very excited that I get to celebrate today by learning Chinese ink and wash painting, and shadow play with Chinese artists to mark Chinese New Year together. In the past three months, I have visited several cities in China to promote U.K.-China relations and got first-hand experience of different local cultures and traditions. I'm always inspired by the good that partnerships between British and Chinese people bring. The year 2020 has been very unusual and difficult for all of us. In the face of the global challenges from COVID-19, the U.K. is focused on working with our international partners, including China, to strengthen the global response to the virus.

We can all take inspiration from the spirit of the ox in the Chinese zodiac and be reminded of the importance of bravery and determination when overcoming our shared challenges. The ox also symbolizes vitality and prosperity. And we should use this to remind us that 2021 is a year filled with hope. The challenges and difficulties, though still ahead, will be overcome. I believe the U.K. and China will continue to inherit the spirit of the ox to build strong relations between our people and work together to tackle climate change, improve global health, and lead the global economic recovery.

I wish you the very best!

I wish you and your loved ones a happy Chinese New Year!

笔记示范

1. The importance of the Chinese New Year:

A. To celebrate.

B. To reflect.

C. To look ahead.

2. Her three-month experience in China and U.K.-China relations:

A. Joint response to COVID-19.

3. The spirit of the ox in the Chinese zodiac:

A. Bravery and determination.

B. Vitality and prosperity.

C. Their extended meanings to the prospects of 2021 U.K.-China cooperation.

4. New Year greetings.

第五章　口译的译前准备与预测

练习一

中国国家主席习近平会见英国四十八家集团俱乐部主席斯蒂芬·佩里

预测内容

　　1. 英国四十八家集团俱乐部。

　　2. 俱乐部主席斯蒂芬·佩里的情况。

　　3. 谈话内容：中英贸易、中英关系、当前形势等。

译前示范准备（预测内容 1）

　　英国四十八家集团俱乐部是一个致力于推动中英贸易关系发展的民间机构。1993 年，佩里任该俱乐部主席。他的父亲杰克·佩里被誉为中英关系的"破冰者"。1953 年，时任伦敦出口公司董事长的老佩里和其他 15 名英国工商界代表突破了西方对中国的封锁，访问北京，开启了最早的贸易对话。这个"破冰之旅"为以老佩里为首的 48 名英国商界人士访问中国奠定了基础，这就是英中贸易四十八家集团的前身。1991 年，该集团改名为英国四十八家集团俱乐部。多年来，该俱乐部在改善中国与西方关系，尤其是在中英关系方面做出了卓越贡献。如今的四十八家集团俱乐部拥有 600 多名中英两国个人或机构成员，涵盖商业、文化、外交、学术等多个领域。该俱乐部以平等互利为信条，向所有致力于积极建设中英关系的人开放，并为他们提供交流平台。2008 年，四十八家集团俱乐部成立青年破冰者组织，旨在促进两国年轻人之间的交流。

附录：口译音频实录

练习二

中国驻英国大使馆刘晓明大使在官邸同英国约克公爵安德鲁王子共庆新春

预测内容

　　1. 中国驻英国大使馆刘晓明大使情况。

　　2. 英国约克公爵安德鲁王子情况以及他与中国的关系。

　　3. 谈话内容：中国春节、美食、中英关系等。

译前示范准备（预测内容2）

　　安德鲁王子是英女王伊丽莎白二世的次子，1986年被封为约克公爵，现担任英国国际贸易及投资的特别代表。2014年，安德鲁王子创立了全球性的创业孵化公益平台Pitch@Palace，中文名为"龙门创将"，并在全球十多个国家和地区设有分赛区。2015年10月，中国国家主席访英开启了中英关系"黄金时代"。次年，英国约克公爵安德鲁王子造访中国，向主席表达了希望"龙门创将"落地中国的意愿，这为"龙门创将"在中国的落地奠定了坚实基础。作为中英关系"黄金时代"下的"黄金果实"，"龙门创将"既是"一带一路"背景下中英创新合作的重要平台，也是中英建交45周年之际对中英友谊的献礼，得到了两国高层的大力支持。2017年5月，首届"龙门创将"全球创新创业大赛·中国赛区总决赛（Pitch@Palace China 1.0）在北京圆满落幕。2018年6月1日，第二届"龙门创将"全球创新创业大赛·中国赛区总决赛（Pitch@Palace China 2.0）于北京举行，安德鲁王子出席了本次决赛。安德鲁王子一直致力于汇聚各领域最具影响力的行业领袖，为创业者提供强有力的创业支持，加强各国之间的互助与合作。

第六章　口译笔记

练习一

1） I would like to take this opportunity to thank our Chinese host, for your gracious hospitality and considerate arrangements. One of the purposes of our visit was to make friends, and I am very pleased to find that we are among friends wherever we go. This trip is an extremely rewarding one because we're convinced that our Chinese partner is well ready to cooperate with us and a promising future is waiting for us.

2) I feel honored to come here on my first visit to your beautiful city. This is a happy and memorable occasion for me personally as well as for all the members of my delegation. I would like to take this opportunity to express our sincere thanks to our host for your earnest invitation and gracious hospitality we have received since we set foot on this charming land. May the friendship tie between our two peoples be further developed and consolidated.

3) Can I start by saying how delighted I am to welcome the Shanghai teachers to the Department for Education for the opening ceremony of the England-China teacher exchange. This exchange is perhaps the most valuable education initiative undertaken by our government over the past few years. In years to come, I hope people will look back on it as a turning point which transformed the teaching of mathematics in this country.

4) It's a great pleasure to see so many past and future Chevening scholars here this evening. You are all most welcome. We have gathered tonight to celebrate education, and I'd like to begin with the old English proverb that "Education is not the answer to the question. Education is the means to the answer to all questions".

5) On behalf of all members of the International Publishers Association, I want to extend my sincere congratulations to you on the occasion of the China Youth Publication International (CYPI) London's tenth anniversary. In the short time since the CYPI was founded, we have watched with admiration as this ambitious venture has achieved great things, emerging as a symbol of the international impulse that drives modern Chinese

publishing. It is in everyone's interest that the world has access to the narrative of Chinese culture, and vice versa. The Chinese publishing industry and CYPI in particular are leading the charge in this endeavor, and I wish you every continued success for the future.

练习二

1） 各位使节，明天就是中国的中秋佳节，这个节日象征着团圆与美满。在这里，我要向在座的各位致以衷心的祝福。希望大家利用今天的机会，品味中秋，感受新时代的中国！

2） 我为能在北京接待您和您的家人而深感荣幸。希望你们在这过得愉快。我代王经理向您问候，他因不能前来而深感抱歉。您若愿意的话，可以下榻地处市中心的北京饭店，从饭店开车30分钟可到我们公司。住宿费由我们公司承担。

3） 我们为能够在此接待史密斯教授率领的伦敦大学代表团而深感高兴和荣幸。我谨代表我校的全体师生向你们表示热烈的欢迎，并希望你们在此过得愉快。在你们今后几天的访问中，我们希望能够有机会学习你们的办学经验，同时也希望我们两校之间进一步加强交流与合作。

4） 我谨代表组委会，感谢在座的各位出席本次国际大会。参加大会的有500多位外国代表和来宾，这对我们来说是巨大的鼓励和支持。北京是一个充满活力的现代化都市，又是一座历史文化名城，希望大家在会后可以花一些时间游览北京。最后，我希望大家在北京过得愉快，并预祝此次会议圆满成功。

5） 我代表天津市政府向前来出席"天津周"各项活动的嘉宾，致以最诚意的问候和最热烈的欢迎。天津作为一个港口城市，资源丰富，人才济济。此次活动旨在带动渤海湾地区的经济发展，为国内外企业带来无限商机。祝愿"天津周"活动取得圆满成功！

练习三

A Speech by Her Majesty the Queen at the China State Banquet, 2015[1]

Mr. President,

Prince Philip and I are delighted to welcome you and Madame Peng to Buckingham Palace this evening.

Your visit to the United Kingdom marks a milestone in this unprecedented year of cooperation and friendship between the United Kingdom and China, as we celebrate the ties between our two countries and prepare to take them to ambitious new heights.

The United Kingdom and China have a warm and longstanding friendship. Prince Philip and I recall with great fondness our visit to China almost 30 years ago, where we were privileged to experience your country's rich history and culture, including the Great Wall, the Forbidden City, and the Terracotta Warriors: all unforgettable memories of China's ancient civilization.

Yet it was China's desire to shape a new future which captivated us the most. We were struck by the energy and enthusiasm with which China's leaders were forging ahead with a new and ambitious future for the Chinese people; and I well recall our discussions with the late paramount leader Mr. Deng Xiaoping, who was foremost among these leaders in setting a clear direction for China with his policy of reform. It was also Mr. Deng's visionary concept of One Country Two Systems which opened the way for the return of Hong Kong to Chinese sovereignty under the Sino-British Joint Declaration.

Almost 30 years later, Mr. Deng's vision has borne remarkable fruit. Rapid economic growth and development has transformed the lives of people across China and lifted hundreds of millions out of poverty: a huge and historic achievement with far-reaching positive effects on people's lives.

---

1 From The Royal Household website.

I was delighted that my grandson Prince William was able to witness these changes during his first visit to China earlier this year. Like myself and Prince Philip, he visited not only your great cities of Beijing and Shanghai but also the beautiful province of Yunnan, and saw at first-hand the strong connections which bind our two countries together, be they in culture, education, or business.

Mr. President, the relationship between the United Kingdom and China is now truly a global partnership. We have much reason to celebrate the dynamic, growing economic relationship between our countries as well as our success in working together to address pressing international challenges.

We have, this year, marked the 70th anniversary of the foundation of the United Nations. Today the world faces challenges which call for collaboration between the nations: conflict and terrorism; poverty and ill-health; conservation and climate change. As permanent members of the United Nations Security Council, Britain and China are stewards of the rules-based international system, and we have a responsibility to cooperate on these issues which have a direct bearing on the security and prosperity of all our peoples.

This global partnership is supported by an expanding network of links between the people of our two countries, which are essential in building mutual understanding and friendship, while we welcome the increasing numbers of Chinese tourists, students, and business visitors to the United Kingdom.

Mr. President, your visit is a defining moment in this very special year for our bilateral relationship. I am confident that it will serve to highlight the sincerity and warmth of our friendship and to strengthen relations between our countries for many years to come.

Ladies and gentlemen, I ask you to rise and drink a toast to the President and Madame Peng and to the people of China.

练习四

习近平主席在上海合作组织青岛峰会欢迎宴会上的祝酒辞[1]

青岛国际会议中心，2018年6月9日

尊敬的各位同事，

各位来宾，

女士们，先生们，朋友们：

大家晚上好！

很高兴同各位相聚在黄海之滨的山东青岛。首先，我谨代表中国政府和中国人民，并以我个人的名义，对来华出席上海合作组织成员国元首理事会会议的各国领导人和国际组织负责人，对各位来宾，表示热烈的欢迎！

山东是孔子的故乡和儒家文化的发祥地。儒家思想是中华文明的重要组成部分。儒家倡导"大道之行，天下为公"，主张"协和万邦，和衷共济，四海一家"。这种"和合"理念同"上海精神"有很多相通之处。"上海精神"坚持互信、互利、平等、协商、尊重多样文明、谋求共同发展，强调求同存异、合作共赢，在国际上获得广泛认同和支持。

在"上海精神"的引领下，本组织不仅在安全、经济、人文等合作领域取得丰硕成果，在机制建设方面也迈出历史性步伐。如今，上海合作组织拥有8个成员国、4个观察员国、6个对话伙伴，是维护地区安全、促进共同发展、完善全球治理的重要力量。

青岛是世界著名的"帆船之都"，许多船只从这里扬帆起航、追逐梦想。明天，我们将在这里举行上海合作组织扩员后的首次峰会，全面规划本组织未来的发展蓝图。

让我们以青岛峰会为新的起点，高扬"上海精神"的风帆，齐心协力，乘风破浪，共同开启上海合作组织发展新征程！

现在，我提议，大家共同举杯，

1　来自中国政府网网站。

为青岛峰会圆满成功,

为各国发展繁荣、人民幸福安康,

为上海合作组织的美好明天,

为各位来宾和家人的健康,

干杯!

第七章　句子口译技巧

练习二

1) I particularly want to pay tribute, not only to those who prepared the magnificent dinner, but also to those who have provided the splendid music.

2) In the spirit of frankness which I hope will characterize our talk this week, let us recognize these points at the outset.

3) What brings us together is that we have common interest, which transcends those differences.

4) While we cannot close the gulf between us, we can try to bridge it so that we may be able to talk across it.

5) What is the world? In a personal sense, I think of my eldest daughter whose birthday is today.

6) 中国有34个省级行政区,包括23个省、5个自治区、4个直辖市和2个特别行政区。

7) 据世界卫生组织的报告显示,到2020年,世界老年人口将超过10亿,其中7亿人生活在发展中国家。

8) 中国外交的辉煌成就,首先归功于党的领导,这是中国外交最根本的政治保障。

9) 我要感谢牛津大学盛情邀请我来参加此次研讨会,让我能和很多年轻学生见面,并分享我的一些想法。

10) 双方要求同存异、聚同化异,以实际行动维护好两国关系发展大局。

练习四

1) This owes much to the settlement worked out between us for the future of Hong Kong.

2) The conscientious efforts of both sides during the past two years have been dedicated to the full and smooth implementation of the Sino-British Joint Declaration.

3) From such contacts come a growing recognition that we have two traditions, but one hope for the future.

4) The climate and environment may be different; yet with an abiding commitment to friendship and development, there will be no obstacles too hard to overcome.

5) I shall tell them that my visit to China represents the fulfillment of a hope which I have cherished for a long time.

6) 我谨代表英国人民，通过您，向中国人民表达我们对中国未来最美好的祝愿！

7) 让我们敞开心扉，不仅要谈论那些机会，还要谈论为了所有公民的利益，我们如何保护这些机会。

8) 直到生命的最后一天，父亲的一生都对我们很有启发。随着年龄的增长，他教会了我们如何有尊严地、幽默地、善良地变老。

9) 创新是第一动力。只有敢于创新、勇于变革，才能突破世界经济发展的瓶颈。

10) 中国经过艰苦努力，全年经济实现2.3%的增长，这是来之不易的。

练习六

1) Nature is angry. And we fool ourselves if we think we can fool nature, because nature always strikes back. Consider the last few months, July—the hottest month ever, June through August—the hottest summer in the Northern Hemisphere ever, and the years 2015 to 2019—the five hottest

years on the books ever. Our warming Earth is issuing a chilling cry: Stop. If we don't urgently change our ways of life, we jeopardize life itself. How we grow food, use land, fuel our transport, and power our economies matter a lot to our environment. We need to link climate change to a new model of development—a fair globalization—with less suffering, more justice and harmony between people and the planet.

2) Over the past decades, there are three major pollution problems. First, with the development of industry, more and more factories have been built and have sent smoke and poisonous gases out, which have polluted the air. At the same time, the increasing number of cars also adds to air pollution. Second, farmers use chemical fertilizers to increase production and pesticides to kill pests. When rain flows with these poisonous chemicals to rivers, water is polluted. The third problem is noise pollution, which is becoming more and more serious. Loud noise can make people sick and even drive them mad. Therefore, air pollution, water pollution, and noise pollution are the main problems affecting people's lives.

3) 植树造林是中国采取的保护环境的措施之一。1979年，中国把3月12日定为国家植树日。在这一天，来自各行各业的数百万中国人会带着铁锹、水桶和树苗，走出户外去绿化家乡。其中一个很好的例子是中国北方的"绿色长城"，也被称为"三北防护林工程"，即在中国西北、华北和东北地区建设人工森林，形成防风带，以阻止戈壁沙漠的扩张。该计划始于1978年，计划在2050年左右完成。

4) 塞罕坝林场位于河北省，与内蒙古接壤，是中国生态保护项目的典型范例。自1962年建场以来，三代塞罕坝人接续努力，在极其恶劣的自然条件和生态环境下建成了世界上面积最大的人工林，创造了沙漠变绿洲、荒原变林海的绿色奇迹。他们用了55年的时间将这个只有一棵树的地方变成了美丽的森林公园，即塞罕坝国家公园，创造了令世人为之惊叹的奇迹。

第八章 数字口译

练习六

1) 17,800
2) 986,296
3) 350,450
4) 9 billion
5) 1,500
6) 300 million
7) 74.34 billion
8) 17.84 billion
9) 67.5 billion
10) 242,500
11) 66 million
12) 10 million
13) 800 million
14) 1.3 billion
15) 65 billion
16) 4 trillion
17) 260 million
18) 5,260
19) 0.45 billion
20) 1,199,810

练习七

1）三千六百
2）三万
3）五万六千
4）九万八千八百八十八
5）十万
6）四十万
7）五百万
8）九百六十万
9）两千万
10）三亿
11）十亿
12）二十亿
13）四百亿
14）两百八十多亿
15）一千亿
16）两万亿
17）82.46 亿
18）743.4 亿
19）九十亿
20）一万七千八百

练习九

1）Canada has a total area of 9.9 million square kilometers, making it the second largest country in the world (after Russia).

2）Canada that touches the Pacific, Arctic, and Atlantic oceans features the longest coastline in the world, stretching 202,080 kilometers.

3）Canada has more lakes than the rest of the world combined. At last count, there may be as many as 2 million, with 563 lakes larger than 100 square kilometers.

4) Canada's video game sector is a 4.5-billion-dollar industry. It is estimated that there are over 48,000 people who already work in Canada's gaming industry and this number will grow by 25% in the next two years.

5) By the end of 2019, Canada's cumulative investment in China was nearly $11 billion, and China's investment in Canada exceeded CA$18 billion.

6) Chinese and Canadian firms signed 56 deals worth more than $1.2 billion at a ceremony on Thursday.

7) Currently, more than 200,000 Chinese students are studying in Canada, and more than 1.5 million tourists travel between the two countries every year.

8) China is Canada's second largest trading partner. The scale of bilateral trade has kept expanding from $150 million 50 years ago to $74 billion in 2019, a nearly 500-fold increase.

9) 自 1978 年中国实行改革开放以来，估计有超过 8 亿人摆脱了贫困。

10) 中国已建成分别覆盖超过 9 亿人的基本养老保险体系和超过 13 亿人的基本医疗保险体系。

11) 2019 年，中国国内生产总值同比增长 6.1%，总量达到约 14.4 万亿美元，人均 GDP 突破 1 万美元。

12) 作为一个拥有 14 亿多人口的发展中大国，中国实现了比较充分就业。

13) 2017 年，中国在境外设立企业超过 3 万家，在海外劳务人员约 100 万，留学生约 137 万。

14) 2019 年全年，中国公民出境旅游人数超过 1.55 亿人次，同比增长 3.3%。

15) 2018 年，中国新能源汽车新增 125 万辆，这一数字在全球遥遥领先。

16) 预计未来 15 年，中国进口商品和服务将分别超过 30 万亿美元和 10 万亿美元。

练习十一

1) Manchester is the cradle of the Industrial Revolution. In recent years, it has continuously adjusted its economic structure, promoted its revitalization and development, and become a financial and commercial center in the northern part of England. Its economy is robust, diverse, and growing. With over 124,000 businesses, it is already a great place to live and work for many people. Manchester stands ready to open wider to welcome worldwide investors and strengthen economic cooperation with China, India, and other emerging markets.

2) Fundamental changes in the global economy have occurred in the last 20 years because of e-commerce. The revolution in e-commerce is now a major component of world trade, from some of the world's largest corporations, like Alibaba and Amazon, to thousands of small companies who have never before been able to trade internationally. Services are now a larger part of the world economy than ever before and more easily traded across borders thanks to the Internet and digital telecommunications.

3) 香港自回归祖国以来，一直是世界上最自由、最开放、最繁荣、最具活力的地区之一。多年来，香港作为全球金融中心之一，在国际金融市场上占据独特的重要地位。它具有其他国际金融中心不具备的"'一国两制'、贯通中西"的独特优势。截至2019年末，香港股市总市值接近5万亿美元，仅次于纽约、上海和东京。香港是亚洲最大的国际基金管理中心和国际私人财富管理中心，资产管理规模超过3万亿美元。香港还是重要的国际银行业中心，全球排名前100的银行中有70多家在香港营业，资产规模超过3万亿美元。

4) 华为创立于1987年，是全球领先的信息与通信基础设施和智能终端提供商。目前，我们约有19.4万名员工，业务遍及170多个国家和地区，服务30多亿人。华为在英国将近20年，创造了2.6万个就业机会，并建立了6个研究中心，雇佣了数百名研究人员。我们致力于把数字世界带给每个人、每个家庭、每个组织，构建万物互联的智能世界。

练习十二

Celebrating Trading Opportunities Between China and the U.K.[1]

Ladies and gentlemen,

I am delighted to be here today in Xi'an at the opening ceremony of the Third Silk Road International Exposition. I want to thank our hosts for naming the U.K. as this year's country of honor.

Trade between our two nations has never been stronger. In the 46 years since we established full ambassadorial relations, our trade has bloomed. You're now our second-largest export market outside Europe and our second largest source of goods imports. The U.K. is now the home of much Chinese investment in Europe. From London's iconic Canary Wharf, to Wolverhampton Wanderers and Aston Villa football clubs, to offshore wind in Scotland—Chinese investment is fueling the U.K.

Indeed, the U.K. is almost uniquely open to investment and trade. London ranks as one of the world's largest financial centers, and it's the world's largest clearing center for the renminbi outside China. The U.K. is the world's second-largest services exporter and we're friendly towards business and investment—the World Bank independently ranks us seventh in the world for the ease of doing business.

You can see this for yourself—we have over 50 U.K. companies at this event, from infrastructure and engineering, to financial and professional services, to health care, education, and culture. They're part of the largest U.K. delegation ever to visit Northwest China—over 200 strong. And this is about

---

[1] Baroness Fairhead speaks at the opening of the Third Silk Road International Exposition on May 11, 2018. From Department for International Trade website.

far more than just London and Beijing. We have over 58 active partnerships regionally.

I'm pleased to be accompanied by a delegation led by the Lord Provost of Edinburgh, which is celebrating its sister city relationship with Xi'an. In the past few years, our relationship with Xi'an in particular has gone from strength to strength. In the last year alone, we've seen a highly-successful joint venture between Queen Mary University in London and North West Polytechnical University and the city of Liverpool is hosting your world-famous Terracotta Warriors. In fact, the exhibition is so successful that the Museum has extended its opening hours to let people from across the United Kingdom experience these historic pieces in person. I would like to express my thanks again to the people of Shaanxi for their generosity in sharing these particularly precious items. And these are just a few examples. We've worked together on agriculture, advanced manufacturing, technology, intellectual property, health care, life sciences, and culture, creativity, and education.

I think that's very apt—Shaanxi and the U.K. represent two ends of the Belt and Road Initiative. Shaanxi is the starting place of the ancient Silk Road. The U.K. is now the most westerly point of the Belt and Road, with the first train from Yiwu arriving in London in 2017—a journey across 9 countries, 2 continents, and 7,500 miles. But we want the relationship between Edinburgh and Shaanxi, and the U.K. and China, to grow even stronger.

It has been two and a half years since President Xi Jinping's state visit, when our leaders declared the "Golden Era" of relations between the United Kingdom and China. Earlier this year our Prime Minister, Theresa May, visited China and launched a new chapter in that "Golden Era". We are already working together on President Xi's Belt and Road Initiative. And our export credits agency, U.K. Export Finance, has affirmed its capacity to support up to £25 billion of new business in key Belt and Road markets. Right here in Xi'an our visa application center has seen a marked increase in applications, and the British Embassy was pleased to attend the launch, earlier this week, on Monday, of Tianjin Airlines, a direct flight between Xi'an and London. It's going to be easier for us to travel, to study, to work, and to trade.

Indeed, trade and mutual economic benefit is at the heart. Our Prime Minister welcomed President Xi's commitment to free trade in his Boao speech last month, and subsequent confirmation of the start of the London-Shanghai Stock Connect. We support this vision of openness, greater interconnectivity, and trade, across the region and across the world.

We are a natural trading nation and a globally-minded country. As you all know, the U.K. will soon be leaving the European Union. So, I want to reassure all of you that we're not turning away from the world. Indeed, far from it—we are a naturally globally-facing nation, and that is how we intend to stay. We will continue to work actively with our friends and partners in China and across the world. Our relationship with China, and our trade with China, is a natural part of that.

So, I'm really pleased to celebrate and support the Third Silk Road International Exposition. It is a great opportunity to showcase the very best of British goods and services, a great showcase of the opportunities from trade between our countries, and a great symbol of our growing ties—the "Golden Era" 2.0.

Thank you.

练习十三

中国驻新西兰大使吴玺在"三城经济联盟"峰会活动上的致辞[1]

2019年5月20日

尊敬的戈夫市长,

张硕辅书记,

戈雷尔副市长,

女士们,先生们:

非常高兴同大家相聚在"三城经济联盟"峰会,并共同庆祝广州和奥克兰缔结友好城市30周年。

广州、奥克兰和洛杉矶都是独具特色的城市,三个城市都位于亚太地区,都是各自国家工业、贸易和技术领域的佼佼者,都拥有活力、开放和包容。

广州一直处于中国改革开放的前沿,以改革创新精神、优良的基础设施和发达的工业享誉全球。与此同时,通过加强与周边地区的贸易、资本、基础设施以及人文互联互通,广州已成泛珠三角地区发展的主要引擎之一。

自2014年加入"三城经济联盟"以来,广州尝试将这种联通从亚洲扩展到大洋洲和北美地区,以进一步促进共同发展和繁荣,造福更多人民。互联互通是开展合作的基础,这与"一带一路"倡议的指导原则和合作理念一脉相承。"一带一路"合作的成功开展表明,地理距离已不再是合作的障碍。

改革开放以来,中国不断融入国际社会,坚定支持自由贸易和多边主义,同很多国家一起享受到开放带来的诸多好处。但近年来,保护主义和单边主义抬头,自由贸易体制面临许多不确定、不稳定因素。美国最近采取的提高贸易壁垒的举措与该国支持自由贸易的传统相左。这些举措损害了中国的利益,违背了自由贸易的原则和精神,给世界经济带来了风险,

---

[1] 来自中国驻新西兰大使馆网站。

最终也会损害美国自身利益。

历史已充分证明，全球化和多边主义是大势所趋，合作是应对挑战的唯一正确选择，是我们实现发展强大的必由之路。正如习近平主席指出的，"世界经济的大海，你要还是不要，都在那儿，是回避不了的。想人为切断各国经济的资金流、技术流、产品流、产业流、人员流，让世界经济的大海退回到一个一个孤立的小湖泊、小河流，是不可能的，也是不符合历史潮流的。"

中国将坚持走和平发展道路，推动建设相互尊重、公平正义、合作共赢的新型国际关系。中国将继续深化改革，扩大开放。一个更加开放和繁荣的中国对包括新西兰和美国在内的世界各国，都意味着更多的机遇。

太平洋是连接我们每个人的桥梁。让我们携手努力，通过加强跨太平洋贸易、政策、基础设施、金融和人文互联互通，进一步加强合作，更好造福各方。

再次祝贺本次会议取得圆满成功！

谢谢大家！

第九章　习语口译

练习二

1）to kill the goose that lay golden eggs

2）to strike while the iron is hot

3）to fish in the air

4）Don't wash your dirty linen in public.

5）to play with fire

6）six of one and half a dozen of the other

7）Where there is smoke, there is fire.

8）the apple of one's eye

9）Still waters run deep.

10）The spirit is willing but the flesh is weak.

11）追悔莫及

12）人山人海

13）狗仗人势

14）塞翁失马，焉知非福。

15）巧妇难为无米之炊

16）像热锅上的蚂蚁

17）三思而后行

18）岁月不待人

19）本末倒置

20）海内存知己，天涯若比邻。

练习四

1）There are arguments to be made on both sides, but I would say people who live in glass houses should not throw stones.

2）Oxford really blew his mind. He loved the feeling of the place, and he loved the people.

3）Do not look back; look ahead. Keep your shoulder to the wheel, your feet on the ground. That is what I have done; it is how I have lived my life so far.

4）She may give the impression that she wears the trousers but it's Tim who makes the final decisions.

5）The show was really good. The music was great and the costumes were out of this world.

6）I don't really like going out to bars anymore. I only go once in a blue moon.

7）We missed our flight to Paris because the connecting flight was late and to add insult to injury, they made us pay for a new ticket as if it was our fault!

8）It costs an arm and a leg to watch local teams, so supporting England abroad must cost a fortune.

9）Mum had to work extra hard to make ends meet so she spent more and more time away from home, and Mary came in more often to help.

10）Denise is definitely burning the candle at both ends—she's been getting to the office early and staying very late to work on some big project.

11）这个世界上，各种话题层出不穷、花样翻新，就像太平洋和印度洋上的浪花，一时引人耳目，转瞬归于平寂。

12）自1997年香港回归以来，中国政府始终坚定不移、全面准确贯彻"一国两制"方针，取得举世公认的成就。

13）在经济全球化深入发展的今天，弱肉强食、赢者通吃是一条越走越窄的死胡同，包容普惠、互利共赢才是越走越宽的人间正道。

14）借口《中英联合声明》对香港事务说三道四、横加干涉，毫无道理可言，不仅违背"一国两制"，也违反国际关系基本准则。

15）中国古代思想家孔子说："与朋友交，言而有信。"政治互信是两国关系健康发展的重要保障。

16）"观今宜鉴古，无古不成今。"历史是一面镜子，它照亮现实，也照亮未来。了解历史、尊重历史才能更好地把握当下，以史为鉴、与时俱进才能更好地走向未来。

17）对于中美双方来说，只要我们坚定方向、锲而不舍，就一定能推动中美新型大国关系建设得到更大发展，更好地造福两国人民和各国人民。

18）改革开放40年来，中国人民自力更生、发愤图强、砥砺前行，依靠自己的辛勤和汗水书写了国家和民族发展的壮丽史诗。

19) 逆水行舟，不进则退。面对新的形势，新兴市场国家和发展中国家需要同舟共济、坚定信心，联手营造有利发展环境，努力实现更大发展，为世界经济增长做出更大贡献。

20) "大道之行也，天下为公。"当今世界，各国相互依存、休戚与共，我们要顺势而为，推动构建以合作共赢为核心的新型国际关系，打造人类命运共同体。

练习六

1) In 2015, our charity walk marked the First Year of U.K.-China Cultural Exchange, and this year we have chosen culture again as the focus of our walk. Why? Because culture connects people, while sometimes different politics and languages divide. We can all be inspired by a beautiful piece of music or dance; we can all appreciate the skill and thought of a painting or sculpture; we can all look at mountains and lakes, sunrises and sunsets, flowers and birds, and feel a connection; we can all share in the excitement of a sporting race or contest.

2) These are not easy times in international relations, which is why we should focus more on what connects us and less on what divides us. Not because what divides us is not important but because we have so much more in common than what divides us. These charity walks are a joint expression of friendship by my wife and I. My wife loves China, the country of her birth, and is incredibly proud of it, but she has also grown to respect and appreciate the U.K. for the opportunities given to her. I also love Britain, where I have lived for half my life, and I am incredibly proud of this country. But since meeting my wife in 2011, I have grown in respect and appreciation for China. I am proud to be called a son-in-law of China. I am proud to have been appointed as a visiting professor at this great university. This is why we walk to promote friendship and understanding especially between the U.K. and China.

3）中华文明是在同其他文明不断交流互鉴中形成的开放体系。从历史上的佛教东传、"伊儒会通",到近代以来的"西学东渐"、新文化运动、马克思主义和社会主义思想传入中国,再到改革开放以来的全方位对外开放,中华文明始终在兼收并蓄中历久弥新。

4）世界上找不到第二座像扬州这样的城市,她与2 500年的大运河一起诞生并成长。自古以来,扬州的历史就与大运河的历史和发展交织在一起,创造了独特的运河城市文化。历史上,中国文化曾借助大运河扩大了世界影响力。今天的扬州仍在以大运河为情感纽带,与世界文化交汇、经济交融,使越来越多的人了解大运河畔的中国故事。如今,扬州正在成为世界名城。

练习七

Speech for the Commemoration of 40 Years of China's Reform and Opening-up[1]

I first want to express my profound and sincere thanks for the invitation to speak here this morning. It is an enormous privilege for a Western scholar to be able to join with you in celebrating 40 years of China's reform and opening-up.

The main part of my career has been devoted to exploring and explaining globalization. It is a controversial topic in the West, often denounced as the new imperialism. You in China have an independent and more balanced view.

Deng Xiaoping's preparations for and follow-up to the epoch making announcements of the Third Plenary Session of the 11th Communist Party Central Committee could be seen as a showcase for globalization. He visited Japan and Singapore beforehand, and, immediately after, when normal relations with the United States were resumed, he was entertained by President Jimmy Carter in the White House.

---

1 Speech by Martin Albrow on December 11, 2018, at Central Hall Westminster, London.

There is indeed a strong case for arguing that it was China's opening-up which gave the kick-start to Western globalization. The two biggest global corporations of the time, General Motors and Coca Cola, arrived in China at that very time to talk of joint ventures. It was not until 1983, 4 years later, that globalization, as the drive for global markets, became the hot topic for Western business.

Opening-up has never been either the victim or the child of Western globalization. It has always been based on socialism with Chinese characteristics, on ongoing reform of every sector of society, and on win-win relations with other countries. This means it works for individuals as well as for countries. Think of all those Chinese people who have studied, worked, and lived in other countries and returned to help build a better future for their fellow citizens. Opening-up has meant going out too.

I was reminded of that vividly on being asked to give an interview on globalization by your CCTV in Beijing a few years ago. The interviewer and I had an informal conversation as a prelude to the broadcast. I was astonished to learn that he had taken a qualification at the School of Journalism in Cardiff University in Wales that I had helped to establish over 30 years before.

Cardiff was also the base for my earliest personal experience of opening-up. In the 1980s I directed the Center for Population Policies there. Every year we welcomed two or three officials sent by the Family Planning Commission of China for mid-career training.

I and my wife, who also lectured in the Center, were the guests of the Commission for a two-week tour of its program in November, 1987. Its officials took infinite care to inform us fully and to answer our questions as well as to entertain us with the utmost generosity. But we were also taken to villages, to meet with their citizens and the program workers, and to observe the grass roots operations of the system.

That experience made a huge impression on us because we learned at first-hand that opening-up began with the countryside and not with Western foreign investment. Deng's own explanation of that policy to a foreign audience in the June of that year was already published in a book that I was able to bring back home and that is in my hand at this moment. This is what he said:

"We introduced reform and the open policy first in the economic sphere, beginning with the countryside. Why did we start there? Because that is where 80% of China's population lives... If the peasants did not shake off poverty, it would mean that China remained poor."

There are vivid lessons there for us currently in the West today. China's opening-up is based on a much more rounded view of the world than globalization. It implies reciprocity, between peoples and individuals, and the harmonious world within and between cultures as advanced by President Hu Jintao in 2005.

It is a concept being put to work by President Xi Jinping in the Belt and Road Initiative. Developed as his community of shared future for mankind, it can be China's decisive contribution to the world's need for the reform of global governance. In global tasks we can come together in that spirit.

His Excellency Ambassador Liu Xiaoming spoke last week, on receiving the Freedom of the City of London, of the Golden Era of cooperation between China and the U.K. It was he who said "in a global perspective".

To my mind, that takes us beyond simple ideas of Western globalization. Therefore, I hope all would join me here, on this occasion of the celebration in the U.K. of the anniversary in expressing thanks to the People's Republic of China and to the Ambassador and all his staff in the Embassy for showing how opening-up works to the benefit of all nations, and us in particular.

Thank you very much.

练习八

中国驻英国大使馆马辉公使在马恩岛华人协会 5 周年庆典上的讲话

马恩岛首府道格拉斯，2018 年 9 月 16 日

女士们、先生们，

亲爱的朋友们：

我和我夫人以及同事很高兴能够来到马恩岛，这个爱尔兰海上的一个古老、神秘、风景如画的岛屿。感谢大家的盛情邀请和热烈欢迎。

我对马恩岛华人协会成立 5 周年致以最热烈的祝贺！自 2013 年 9 月成立以来，该协会一直致力于推动中华文化的传播和争取华人社区的福祉，促进马恩岛与中国之间的经贸联系。感谢你们的努力和奉献！

还有两个星期就是中国的传统节日中秋节和中华人民共和国第 69 个国庆日。对中国人来说，这是两个非常重要的节日。在此，我谨向大家致以节日的问候，祝大家身体健康、生活幸福美满！

自 1949 年中华人民共和国成立至今，69 年间发生了巨大的变化，特别是 1978 年中国开始改革开放以来，变化尤为巨大。中国已经成为世界第二大经济体、最大的工业生产国、最大的贸易进出口国，以及最大的外汇储备国。

改革开放 40 年来，中国国内生产总值按可比价格平均每年增长 9.5%。超过 7 亿中国人摆脱了贫困，占同期全球总脱贫人口的 70% 以上。中国人民过上了小康生活。

在这个过程中，中国已经履行了作为主要国家的责任。从"引进外资"到"中国企业走出去"，从加入世贸组织到"一带一路"倡议，中国为全球和平与发展做出了重要贡献。改革开放不仅深刻改变了中国，也深刻影响了世界，包括马恩岛。

马恩岛和中国地理位置相距遥远，但双方在金融、贸易、文化、旅游、教育等各个领域保持着交流与合作。越来越多的中国企业来岛上开展业务，越来越多的中国游客到这里参观游览。岛上开设了孔子课堂。马恩

岛大学学院和中国的大学正在进行更广泛和更深入的合作。一个典型的例子是马恩岛邮局与华人协会合作推出了2015年的第一张小型张，庆祝中国羊年。这个令人惊艳的小型张就是马恩岛与中国关系的佐证。

马恩岛是一个重要的离岸金融商业中心，拥有独特而丰富的凯尔特人和维京人文化遗产。这里有世界上最古老的蒸汽火车和电车；这里有美丽动人的悬崖风光和乡村景观……不胜枚举！我相信中国和马恩岛之间可以有更多、更深层次的合作。中国驻英国大使馆愿为推动这种合作、增进两国人民的相互了解发挥积极作用。我相信马恩岛华人协会将为中国与马恩岛以及中英之间的合作、文化和民间交流做出更大的贡献。

谢谢！

第十章　口译的应变策略

练习二

1) I want to thank everyone in the NHS front line, as well as care workers and those carrying out essential roles, who selflessly continue their day-to-day duties outside the home in support of us all. I am sure the nation will join me in assuring you that what you do is appreciated and every hour of your hard work brings us closer to a return to more normal times.

2) In reducing threats to health, some of China's past achievements have been spectacular. Using medical doctors, barefoot doctors, practitioners of traditional Chinese medicine, health inspectors, and medical staff at factories, this vast and populous country eradicated smallpox 20 years before the rest of the world. In the 3 years prior to its last case, China administered smallpox vaccine to more than 500 million people. That achievement established an attitude at the WHO that persists today: China can do anything whatsoever it decides to do.

3)《北京市控制吸烟条例》是世界上最严厉的控烟条例之一。从2015年6月1日起，法律规定北京所有的室内公共场所都必须100%禁烟。这包括所有室内工作场所，如餐厅、酒吧、饭店、机场和公共交通工具等。许多室外公共场所也将要求禁烟，如幼儿园、校园和医院。该法律还禁止在大众媒体、公共场所、户外和公共交通工具上发布烟草广告。《北京市控制吸烟条例》意义重大，因为它可以减少非吸烟者接触二手烟的风险，而二手烟是无数健康问题的元凶。

4)人类文明史是一部抗击疾病和灾难的历史。病毒没有国界，疫病不分种族。面对来势汹汹的新冠肺炎疫情，各国人民勇敢前行，守望相助，风雨同舟，展现了人间大爱，汇聚起同疫情斗争的磅礴之力。当前，国际抗疫正处于关键阶段，支持世界卫生组织就是支持国际抗疫合作、支持挽救生命。

练习三

WHO Director-General's Opening Remarks at High-Level Video Conference on Belt and Road International Cooperation[1]

June 18, 2020

Your Excellency Wang Yi,

Mr. Achim Steiner,

Excellencies, Ministers, dear colleagues and friends,

The COVID-19 pandemic is the most severe global crisis since the Second World War. More than 8 million cases have now been reported to WHO, and more than 440,000 deaths. The pandemic is accelerating. In the first two months of the outbreak, 85,000 cases were reported to WHO. In the past two months, more than 6 million cases were reported. Lives and livelihoods have been lost. The effects of the pandemic will be felt for years to come.

---

1 From the World Health Organization website.

The two key ingredients for both overcoming the pandemic and supporting the global recovery are national unity and global solidarity. We cannot succeed in a divided world. We appreciate the role China has played in supporting the global response to the pandemic. Since the beginning of the COVID-19 pandemic, China has been active in its assistance to and technical collaboration with other countries. It sent medical teams to many countries and supplies to hundreds of countries, and carried out technical cooperation, sharing its domestic experience. China has also committed to sharing any vaccine it develops as a global good.

Even as we work together to fight the pandemic, we must also listen to the lessons it is teaching us. One of the main lessons is that health is not a luxury, or a reward for development. It is a human right, and a prerequisite for development. Heath and health security are the foundation of sustainable development, peace, and prosperity. This pandemic also reminds us once again that health and health security are not individual, but public and global. The health and health security of the wealthiest is inseparable from that of the most disadvantaged. This is true for individuals, communities, and nations.

In that sense, President Xi Jinping's recent call for a "community of common health for mankind" is very timely, and echoes the opening lines of WHO's Constitution, which sets out a vision for a world in which all people attain the highest possible standard of health. Experience from many countries shows that the best way of achieving that vision is by ensuring all people can access the health services they need, without facing financial hardship—that is the essence of universal health coverage. Achieving universal health coverage depends on building resilient health systems based on strong primary care. Building these systems requires a commitment of political will, resources, and technical expertise and support.

The Belt and Road Initiative has the potential to act as an accelerator for the achievement of universal health coverage and the Sustainable Development

Goals. That's why we say health should be at the center of the Sustainable Development Goals. The world is now realizing that this is the case. It can foster improvements in health and well-being, by supporting economic development and improving the determinants of health in participating countries, and in supporting robust, accessible health systems and public health infrastructure.

China's recent emphasis on the Health Silk Road and the Digital Silk Road points to the importance of innovative forms of cooperation to deal with the challenges we collectively face. The Health Silk Road has the potential to support partnerships to contain COVID-19, to improve infrastructure and access to much needed health services including diagnostic and treatment, and to strengthen health systems under strain because of the pandemic.

WHO is committed to working with China and other partners to turn BRI into a true Health Silk Road and to help realize and define the "community of common health for mankind".

Thank you.